American Haibun & Haiga

stone frog

American Haibun & Haiga

Volume 2

Red Moon Press

stone frog
American Haibun & Haiga Volume 2

Published by
Red Moon Press
PO Box 2461
Winchester VA
22604-1661 USA
redmoon@shentel.net

ISBN 1-893959-19-8

PS593
.H3
S76
2001 x

Cover painting:
"stone frog"
John Polozzolo
8.5" x 11" sumi-e & watercolor
Used by permission.

 **Introduction**

WE BOTH HAVE RECENTLY REREAD *THE TOSA DIARY*, an early Japanese travel journal recounting a sea return of fifty-five days to Kyoto by a court nobleman. The simplicity of the prose, or rather, the effortless flow of sensibility, is most noticeable. An exchange with someone over editing issues with his haibun also recently prompted the thought that most of us writing haibun suffer from issues of narrative style, particularly that we are often too prosaic in manner. Ion Codrescu's "Toward the Mountain Temple," a poetic journey to an ancient Chinese temple and an exploration of the aesthetics of the moment in nature, compares spiritual favorably with *The Tosa Diary* and Basho's *Journey to the Interior* in stylistic approach. Put simply, the manner in which we tell our narrative is as important as the narrative itself, notwithstanding that a good tale is a good tale.

Compare the naive but unsentimental "Hospice" by John Crook to the postmodern tone of "Buying a Soul" by William M. Ramsey. Crook's simply-stated emotion evokes one of life's great challenges and mysteries. Ramsey, a product of contemporary spiritual anxiety, reminds us in a circuitous way about the unsettling malaise that colors our collective horizon. Both are forthright in their sensibility, the one reminiscent of *kokoro*, the Japanese word for heart, the other of the so-called "postmodern condition" of a troubled mind filtered through sentiment. In either case, in either style, pure sentiment touches us deeply.

Although, from another angle, haibun is made up of poetic prose, one should be careful to curtail one's enthusiasm for figurative expression when such expression begins to overshadow the sentiment at the center of a given haibun. We thus might proceed to define our haibun as autobiographical prose heightened by sentiment which incorporates haiku.

The haibun in this second volume of *American Haibun & Haiga* are varied in their chosen approaches to the form but , as you might choose to agree, uniformly exhibit this touchstone of sentiment, even in their most demonstrative narratives. For simplicity of expression consider Yu Chang's moving childhood memory, "Rain," Gene Williamson's epiphany on the persistence of natural beauty, "Home Again," or Ken Hurm's understated hommage to love, "Mother's Day." For deft modern versions of travel diaries consider gop's Thailand exploration of the enigma of spiritual practice and human "frailty," "The Monk's Bowl," John Martone's presentation of deep meditation practice in Vietnam, "Bien Xu," or Brent Partridge's unpretentious account of travel with his mother in out-of-the-way Japan, "The Dawn Road." For narrative focus consider Cherie Hunter Day's adroit weaving of past and present, "The Cabinetmaker's Wish," Margaret Chula's stirring ironic drama of synchronicity, "At Year's End," or Kenneth C. Leibman's humorous encounter with Japanese cuisine, "Okonomiyaki." And for a heightened meditative or measured tone consider Jesse Glass's absorption of a Japanese monk's spiritual example, "Unsen's Stone," Linda Jeannette Ward's elegiac rumination on the Outer Banks, "Small Time," or Gerald George's refined exposition of ecological engagement, "Haibun: Arizona."

These haibun and those standing beside them in this second volume of *American Haibun & Haiga* attest to the vitality of a form so simply started in such an unaffected overture as *The Tosa Diary*. There is nothing but possibility and further possibility in an American and world haibun bound ever-so-lightly by the common strands of human sentiment.

Add to this potent mix the many and diverse styles of American haiku painting, as exemplified in this volume, and it is possible to see that these ancient Japanese arts are flourishing in their new homeland. Contrast the complexity of the painting of Zolo with the simplicity of line of Michael Lyle, the technical mastery of Kuniharu Shimizu with the seeming absence of such of Claudia Graf. In content, too, we have the widest possible range, from the zen-like considerations of Kay F. Anderson to the millennarial thoughts of Marlene Mountain; a grand realization by Jason Fech and the mundanity of the moment of Jean Konnerth. Styles, too, move from the modern abstract expressionism of the collaborations of Croteau and De Gruttola through the naïf realization of Tanya Solorzano, the eastern expressions of Kay F. Anderson and the decidedly western one of Merrill Ann Gonzales. And the media include sumi-e and magic marker, pen and ink, pencil, montage, collage, electronic and even real paint. The result of this breadth of things to say and means to say it is a vitality of the form quite unique in the west, and an exploration of it which is bringing to the palettes of artists one more tool to render the present moment in a manner we all might share. It is this potent combination of word and image which many are finding to be a most satisfying way of coming to, expressing, and sharing their moments.

—*Jim Kacian & Bruce Ross, Editors*

stone frog

Yu Chang

refrigerator

ONE DAY LAST SUMMER, my old refrigerator suddenly quit. When the repairman handed me the culprit, a broken heating element, I happily paid $75 to get my refrigerator back. After that, it worked nicely except for hot days.Then, the motor would moan noticeably but there was no cooling at all. The thought of getting a new one did cross my mind, but I never got around to it.

The fridge's condition got worse in the middle of June this year. "That's it," I said to myself and headed for the mall. When I was removing the postcards and stickers to prepare the old fridge to be trucked away, a yellowed Christmas card caught my eyes. The message inside read, "Merry Christmas! Hope everybody is fine. See you in New York. Love, Siv."

Siv Engstrom grew up in Göteberg, Sweden, but had spent many years abroad both in Europe and in the US by the time I met her. She was the happiest person I'd ever known, and she brought out the best in everyone. Siv particularly loved Britain, so much so that she bought a dilapidated English cottage near Cambridge. Restoration had already begun in the summer of 1988. Siv never made it to New York that year. She made it as far as Lockerbie, Scotland.

> new fridge
> the motor's faint hum
> still there

rain

MANY PEOPLE COMPLAIN about the rain this spring, but the rain has always reminded me of when I was a young child growing up in a small village near Chungking, the wartime capital of China. A rainy day meant there was no need to run to the makeshift air-raid shelter, an old coal mine just beyond the terraced fields of the village. The grassy trails to the shelter could be quite slippery even when dry. One time, after the siren sounded, I ran so fast to try to catch up with everybody else that I fell face down into the field below. Oblivious to the mud all over my body, my mother hugged me after she pulled me up from the rice paddy. I wish now that I had said "I love you," but I just squirmed out of her arms. We were the last ones to get to the shelter. "We are safe now," she smiled.

> deep in the coal mine
> my mother's grip
> tightens

Margaret Chula

At Year's End

ON NEW YEAR'S EVE IN KYOTO, we would invite our friends over to our Japanese-style house to celebrate. We sat on *tatami* mats, tucking our legs under the *kotatsu* to keep warm. Like the Japanese, we ate a meal of *soba* noodles for long life and toasted with *sake* drunk from small cups. Just before midnight, we bundled up and climbed the hill to Matsugasaki Temple. For twelve years, this had been our year-end tradition: to eat, drink, and ring the temple bell. On our last New Year's in Japan, however, something unusual happened.

When we arrived at the temple, people were already lined up. We had all come to ring the bell 108 times to rid the world of the 108 sins. The brass bell is huge—about three feet in diameter—and suspended from an enclosure in the temple courtyard. In front of it, hanging by a strong chain, is an 8-foot long log which you pull back wiht the rope and release, like a battering ram.

A bonfire had been lit in the courtyard and people gathered around it to get warm. As I waited in line, I remembered last year's Daruma doll, which I had brought to burn. This doll is named after a Buddhist saint who vowed to sit in meditation until he became enlightened. He was so determined that he did not give up, even when his legs rotted off. Thus, Daruma symbolizes persistence and endurance. Made of papier-maché, the dolls are round and have no legs. They are weighted so, if they fall over, they right themselves. Daruma dolls come in all sizes. Mine was small, only four inches. In keeping with Japanese tradition, I had bought it on the first day of the New Year, made a vow and drawn in one of his eyes. Only when you have achieved your goal are you allowed to fill in the other eye.

I took the Daruma doll out of my pocket and tossed it into the bonfire. It rolled out. All the Japanese went 'E-eh-e-eee?!' I picked it up and threw it back in. It rolled out again. By this time the Japanese were edging away from me. I picked up my Daruma and threw it into the fire once again. This time it didn't roll out.

at year's end
burning the Daruma
with only one eye

the first snowfall . . .
    searching for something I know
    I'll never find

an ocean away—
I try to draw her closer
with pad & pencil

image & poem::Dennis H. Dutton

collage & poem::Sheila Windsor

mooncrossing

wild geese on the long haul
to the sun

half-moon night –
picturing a face
I've never met

image & poem::Alice Frampton

 **Ion Codrescu**

Towards the Mountain Temple

even through mist
the light finds its way . . .
old temple bell

EARLY MORNING. I open the window and look outside. Suddenly, I feel the moisture which comes into my room. I sip my jasmine tea and at the same time I look at the unfolded map. I take a last look before going towards the mountain temple. The English explanations are written under the Chinese text, which is smaller. To get to the narrow stepping path, I have to walk many hours on a forestry road which goes through two villages and one hamlet. I take my knapsack and say goodbye to the host where I stayed only one night.

parting time—
the host offers the guest
some dewy plums

The road ascends through bamboo, cedar, pine forests and other trees whose names I've forgotten. From time to time, a bird call crosses the mist. I can't see beyond thirty or forty metres. All is gray and it's difficult to distinguish the outline of the trees, plants and rocks. Everything seems unreal. The landscape is like an ink painting where the strong strokes and details have disappeared. It's so quiet that I can hear the dewdrops falling on me from the branches of the tall pines.

lonely mountain road—
how smooth the surface
of the rock

After an hour of climbing, I pause beside a large stone covered with brushwood and I take a swig of the tea I have with me. I find it strange that I have not met anyone—neither travellers nor woodcutters. Time passes while I am gazing at the dense forest, at the branches of the old trees that come together overhead and are so tangled. After some minutes a native approaches and stops his horses, and then invites me to take a seat in his cart. Guessing the place where I will go he pronounces loudly the name of the temple. In my turn, I confirm his intuition and say the same words. His face brightens up and his eyes look at the mountain peak. After some moments, by an interjection, he starts his horses. The sound of the cart and the clatter of hooves are all I hear in the silence of the mountain.

a broken tree—
it's apricot picking time
in my country

After we pass through the two villages the mist begins to rise. The landscape can be seen far away. Unnoticeably cedars and bamboos grow more and more rare. We approach the hamlet. From near the first house two children with their hands up run toward us. They shout the same words. When they notice that in the cart there is a foreigner, their voices fade and they become ashamed. My guide is their father. He stops the horses and raises the children onto the cart, one after another, even though their house is no more than twenty-five or thirty metres away. The faces of the children are radiant. Near their house, I get out from the cart and bend my head to thank my guide. Saying again the name of the temple he points out the place where the path begins through the woods towards the peak.

a gust of wind—
fern leaves cover and uncover
the small white mushroom

Even after the fog disappears, the moisture is on my clothes, plants and the air is full of resin scent. In the sunbeams the dewdrops sparkle. I watch the pine needles, which end with tiny, gleaming dewdrops. Butterflies zigzag around me and I wonder where they stayed hidden until now. Deep in the woods, sometimes loudly, sometimes gently, I hear a woodcutter. Worn down by time and by the steps of countless pilgrims who came to visit the temple, the stone steps are slippery and I must pay attention to each. After half an hour of difficult climbing, I stop for a short while. From far away I can barely hear the waterfall. I continue to climb and the roaring of the water is louder and louder. Unexpectedly, on the narrow path a terrace and a pavilion appear in front of me. I enter the pavilion to sit on a bench and gaze towards the waterfall. Its water is completely white.

              as I
           approach
            to watch
             the waterfall
              a lonely
               bird
                leaves
                 its place

The peaks alternate far away, one by one, like petrified ships floating above a still sea made of white clouds. Suddenly I remember the first Chinese reproductions I saw when I was a teenager. At that time I thought that Chinese mountains are only the fantasy of the painters and that their shapes are not real. Now I have the impression that the mountains I see are a copy of those paintings. I am thinking of Wang Wei, the poet-painter, who wrote in a poem:

        I notice a lonely far away peak
        which vanishes among clouds

As in Wang Wei's poem, this landscape I admire behind the water-fall, far away, a solitary summit is gradually covered, and disappears into the sea of clouds. Sometimes I think that only art copies nature. In this moment I realize that nature imitates art, too.

Near me, another peak, flooded by the light of the sun, is full of green due to the pine trees. In classic Chinese painting a green mountain means stability and a white cloud suggests instability, wandering. To know a mountain you must wander through its paths, woods and rocks, hearing its sounds and voices, watching it from far away or drawing it. Frederick Frank wrote that "Drawing is the discipline by which I constantly rediscover the world. I have learned that what I have not drawn I have never really seen, and that when I start drawing an ordinary thing I realize how extraordinary it is, sheer miracle: the branching of a tree, the structure of a dandelion's seed puff. I discover that among *The Ten Thousand Things* there is no ordinary thing. All that is, is worthy of being seen, of being drawn." I take the brush, the paper and the ink, and paint the landscape. Then I'll go towards the mountain temple.

> the last brush stroke—
> a dewdrop falls
> on my ink sketch

 John Crook

Hospice

I HAVE JUST RETURNED FROM A WEEK AND A HALF in a local hospice to try and get my medication working a little better. Later I was struck by the forebearance and resilience of the patients, some of whom were close to dying. Just before my admission I attended a pantomime put on by the staff, and whilst there I attended a wedding (a remarriage of a divorced couple) and a seventy second birthday party. The nurses were available round the clock, and nothing was too much trouble.

> hospice breakfast—
> last night she cried out
> for her long dead mother

Cherie Hunter Day

The Cabinetmaker's Wish

THE OLD MAHOGANY CHEST OF DRAWERS responds to the lemon oil-soaked scrap of flannel. Stroke by stroke the wood surrenders its grime, restoring the gleam to the grain of the veneer panel on the front of each drawer. The darkened portion of the rag is turned inward to refresh the next area.

heirloom dresser
every scrap from the ragbag
a different story

Inside the drawer the texture changes, its surface is unvarnished; its roughness tugs the cloth. The cabinetmaker's hand-cut joints fastened the sides to the drawer. Not the typical dovetails, but peg-like, placed far apart, showing uneven cuts. The width and depth vary only slightly, but unmistakably unique to each joining. Pencil marks are still evident on the wood where he had numbered the back of each drawer. A corresponding number in the dresser body, just above the glide for each drawer, tells the order of the drawers from top to bottom. The drawers are out of sequence. How many years has it been this way?

pressed into soft wood
at the back of each drawer
his handwriting

At the swipe of the cleaning rag, a rope of cobwebs rolls off the back of the drawer. Something shakes free from a joint at the back of one drawer and rattles to the bottom: a blue-black wire bent in the shape of a long U, a shape that I haven't seen in decades. It is a hairpin from a time when women carefully wrapped and twisted and pinioned their hair into place on top of their heads. I finger my own short-cropped hair.

Outwardly this chest of drawers has always had a masculine appeal. Even the knobs are blunt and unadorned. During my years growing up, the dresser was relegated to an unused corner of the unheated guest bedroom to hold bed linen, an old feather pillow, and a moth-eaten blanket. But in a former life, instead of crude muslin, it held ribbons and lace. Had the cabinetmaker made this dresser for his bride? There is no way to tell; that legacy is erased. I carefully replace the drawers in the pencil-numbered order of the cabinetmaker.

> candle glow—
> he untangles the cascade
> of her scented hair

 **John Dunphy**

Facing the Wall

The polished black granite of the Vietnam Veterans Memorial in Washington DC—popularly known as The Wall—subtly reflects its visitors. While reading the names of the over 58,000 Americans killed during that conflict, we suddenly realize that our images are transposed on those names.

This experience is especially poignant for 'Nam vets seeking the names of those with whom they served. They will never know a closer reunion with their fallen comrades.

> Vietnam Memorial
> aging veterans reflected on
> names of young men

❦

A Captured Memorial

In Ho Chi Minh City—the city Americans will always remember as Saigon—there are two museums devoted to Vietnam War memorabilia: the *War Remnants Museum*, housed in a compound used by the U. S. Information Agency during the war; and the *Revolutionary Museum* in the old Gia Long Palace, built in neoclassical style by the French in 1886, which served as the presidential palace.

In one display in the latter museum there is a plaque inscribed with the names of GIs killed when Vietcong "sappers" (commandos who infiltrated American facilities, often on suicide missions) assaulted the U. S. Embassy during the 1968 Tet Offensive. It had been hung there as a memorial, but was left behind when American forces pulled out of South Vietnam. Since the fall of Saigon in 1975, it had been the property of the opposition.

on a plaque
in the enemy's museum
names of our dead

 **Jeanne Emrich**

Weaver Bottoms ·

IT'S EASY TO GET LOST IN THE WEAVER BOTTOMS. The channeled backwaters of the Upper Mississippi River are unmarked, and as you are drawn on by one mysterious bend after another, by gleaming, lotus-filled bays and heron-sheltering islands studded with wild iris, you can become unmindful of your course. And so, as we started out from Half Moon Landing, we made sure to take note of the landmarks we passed—a spreading willow, driftwood on a sandy shore, a rowboat drawn up at the edge of a pasture, horses that came down to the shore to greet us, heads nodding, tails swishing.

A party of six in three canoes, we at first stayed close together since rain clouds from the night before still threatened to turn us back. But soon we drifted apart, following the allure of cardinal flowers along the shore, a heron winging into the next channel, a snake cutting water with the speed of an Olympic swimmer. After a while, we found ourselves in a sprawling bay, the entire expanse of which was filled with the American Lotus Lily in full bloom. Leaves two and three feet wide, flat on the water or up on two foot stems and flapping in the breeze like ladies' hats. And butter-yellow blossoms, thousands of them, each big as your head.

Soon the way opened to deeper and windier water and we drifted even further apart. Mickey and Marcia headed upriver and disappeared around the next bend, while the rest of us lingered around the lotus bed. When the time came to return to the landing, Mickey and Marcia were still out of sight. Maybe they had found a short cut back to our starting point. Or maybe they were lost. Who could tell where all these channels lead? After a while, they all begin to look alike. It might take days for the two to get back to Half Moon Landing—or maybe they were there already.

We turned back and followed our well-noted landmarks from bend to bend, looking over our shoulder frequently for our wayward friends. We laughed and made bets about who would get there first—Mickey and Marcia or us—but we also wondered how long it would take for a lost couple to find their way out of the backwater maze or for the Coast Guard to go in and find them. Just as we were about to turn around the spreading willow into Half Moon Landing there came a happy shout from behind us. It was Mickey and Marcia pulling up fast. They had not found a shortcut home, but neither had they gotten lost. Unwilling to give up the day's adventure, they had merely given in to the allure of the next bend in the channel and the next after that. Returning the way they'd come, they followed landmarks just as we had—only many more of them. They must have paddled like Voyageurs to catch up with us.

rain clouds lifting . . .
beneath the egret's wings
lotus leaves ripple

 **Judson Evans**

Vigil

AN ANT CIRCLES THE "O" of October—Circus Maximus, carved in granite. A rain of hay drifts at the turning post. The sound of the mowers far above, blue sky of another world . . . The rest of the letters and numbers—your full name/your empty dates: the simple maze of 8, the oxbow of S, the great serpentine without its Versailles, the drained locks of H, its empty artificial waterways. The great moulds emptied of molten summer. The prison yards, pristine canals, the stalls and slave quarters of E.

> laying above you
> tracing the Braille
> of your name

The boys on riding mowers, their fluttering open legged khakis, legs with their dark growth of hair, close cropped summer haircuts consciously ungainly, spoiling to mar the beauty *you* will see to, dead or alive. All the things you would say like a hive at the end of summer.

> teenage mower
> rests his gas can
> on someone's grave

image:Wilfred Croteau
poem:Raffael de Gruttola

signs feeders

tied to lines

release air locks

single morning glory
bobbing on a leafless vine

I bring in firewood

image & poem::Jean Konnerth

image & poem::Stephen Addiss

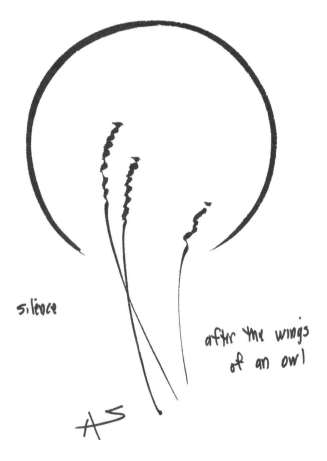

silence

after the wings
of an owl

solstice

collage & poem::Marlene Mountain

 **Liz fenn**

All Systems, Go!

JANUARY. The remainder of a fierce arctic storm lashed out across the whole of the Tug Hill Plateau. Fortunately, road crews had kept up with the ice, so Blanche was able to drive home from work at a slow safe pace. Still, when she arrived at her mailbox to make the turn up into the driveway, she did breathe a loud sigh of relief. But, it was one of very short duration—because, as Blanche carefully began to execute that turn, she lost control of her car. By some miracle, though, her spins and slides averted a thick stand of ice-encased short pines, and her car came to a halt ten feet in off the road.

For a few minutes Blanche was very thankful for her safety and just sat there quietly, in awe and disbelief, after having murmured "oh, dear." Then, she experienced a reality check: "Egad!" she said out loud. "The whole damn driveway up head is a solid mass of ice— shit!" Still, Blanche reasoned she couldn't back her car out, and she knew she had to get home—to warm slippers, to her husband, to a hot meal, and to some lively schmoozing with their St. Bernard, Clown Face . . . Seconds later, then, Blanche switched off the car's engine and lights, let herself out into the elements, and began an inch-by-inch walk the rest of the freezing way home.

But. this proved a NO WAY situation. Blanche executed only two careful little steps and down she fell. She got up, steadied herself, and tried again. Again she fell. "Forget this," she thought out loud while hanging on to a front bumper. "Maybe I'd better just crawl." And so, Blanche promptly got down on all fours and began trying to crawl over the ice and on up the two hundred feet left of driveway to home.

But. This didn't work either. Blanche had no control over her slip and slide crawl, and her face kept smacking directly down onto the numbing ice. "Damn," she thought. "Guess I'll just have to be a snow angel." Immediately, then, Blanche lowered herself until she was flat on her back, spread-eagle over the ice, and she tried to advance and steer by whatever slight wiggles worked. It was slow, tedious going, but eventurally she came within thirty feet of her house. Feeling somewhat successful at last and a great deal less anxious, Blanche now allowed herself a moment's pause, to look up at the kitchen door. To her surprise, she saw her husband and Clown Face standing and jumping around against an adjacent window. From inside, her husband was waving her on as if an officer wanting traffic to speed up and roll along. Blanche laughed aloud, gave a quick short wave in response, and then continued her concise body slides. Finally, when she got within inches of the kitchen door, she heard Clown Face bark and bark between her husband's shouts: "Way t' go! Come on! Come on! Ya made it, babe!" But she hadn't—yet.

The kitchen doorknob was encased in a solid brick of ice, and the entire door frame was cemented shut with ice at least two inches thick. "Oh, great," she thought, "what now?" Then, forgetting about frostbite, Blanche removed her left leather boot and began to chip away furiously at the door's frame while her husband pushed and pounded from the inside. Clown Face kept up his barking, louder than ever, and began jumping higher as if to cheer both of them on. Eventually, the rage of persistent activity succeeded, even though it seemed forever until something finally gave one hundred percent—

a door swings open . . .
the family dog dances
a pee out-of-doors

Stanford Forrester

New Year's Eve

IT WAS NEW YEAR'S EVE and that meant that I had been in Ecuador as a Peace Corps volunteer for over a year now. The town I lived in was only a few kilometers away, but I knew that I needed to pick up the pace to get back before it got really dark. Along the side of the road I passed some farmers' children. They were playing hide and go seek, laughing and calling to each other as they ran between the eucalyptus. They were so enthralled in their game, I walked by them unnoticed. As I kept walking, I had a feeling that the mountains were slowly growing taller and the pine was thickening. After a few minutes the road was no longer a road. It became a path, a path I was the only one on and the only sound I heard was a few crickets chirping in the long esparto grass.

> New Year's Eve—
> even the crickets
> celebrate with a song

Coming closer to town, I was surprised to see three festive young men standing in the middle of the path drinking and telling jokes. They were all dressed in red and each of them wore a devil's mask. They asked me if I wanted a drink and then told me that this was a roadblock. If I paid the devil's toll, they said, I would be allowed to leave all my sins behind and pass into the New Year with a clean slate. So I dropped all my change into their bucket and went on my way home.

> stars falling into
> this evening sky—
> festival lights

 **Alice Frampton**

Black and White

in the sickroom
November sunlight
on the mountain picture

THERE AREN'T MANY SUNNY DAYS LEFT. Mom can leave the blinds open more now. After the intense summer heat, the softer light is a gift. Dad sleeps most of the time, but when he's awake and not struggling for air, he turns to the windows for his entertainment. Living and breathing the seasons has always been his thing. He watches the weather like a hawk, how it affects the animals and their cycles.

replacing Dad's chair
with a hospital bed
—autumn twilight

It's been two years. The rented bed takes up most of the living room, while the oxygen tank, rollaway eating-table, and a few small chairs occupy the corners. In the beginning everyone tiptoed and whispered in this room, but somewhere along the way we adapted to the changes. Outside the weather is shifting. I step to the sliding glass door for a breath of fresh air. Madrona bark and fir boughs, souvenirs of yesterday's wind, freckle the grass. I'll talk to my brother about one last mowing. The giant firs at the edge of the land are swaying gently and the soothing rhythm quiets my pounding heart. I grew up under the shelter of these trees. Forty years ago Dad cleared this lot leaving two strapping sentinels to protect us from strong gales, then positioned the house so that he could keep his eye on nature and the activity around the bay. But today the breeze off the water is blowing in from the north; a sure sign of severe

storms ahead. November's an iffy month; sun one minute, heavy
rain or snow the next. I hear his voice and return to the group. He's
awake and reminiscing once more.

> December tree fall—
> at the windows
> an empty space

❧

Cheeky

IT'S THE LAST BOYS' SOCCER GAME of the season. Standing in mud, ankle
deep, along a sideline where half the student body has littered the
ground with lunchings and sports tape, I meet with other parents to
cheer on our high school's team. Since it's the beginning of
November in British Columbia, my arms are loaded down with an
umbrella, scarf, hat, gloves, and a warm blanket. I also carry a sack-
chair over my shoulder and an insulated coffee mug in one hand.
Having three sons, all of whom play soccer, I'm a pro spectator.

> a few stray drops—
> seagulls position themselves
> for the outcome

My son is on the field stretching his hamstrings before the opening
kick-off. He doesn't want to be reminded that I'm around, but I
catch him looking for me all the same. I set up my chair, close enough
to see all, and settle in. Some parents pace, but after many seasons,
I've relaxed into the role.

> half-time grins
> appearance of the sun
> in the oranges

It's a well played game, with few abuses flung at the referee or between members of the opposing sides. When the final whistle sounds the score is tied one to one. I start to squirm at the prospect of two ten-minute overtimes and a shoot-out. With the extension, tempers flare and everyone braces for the worst.

on the field
best laid plans—
no restrooms

Through it all we finally win and head to the parking lot where our team bus waits. To avoid any confrontations, the parents and coaches gather alongside while the boys pile in. Then, as our players' bus pulls away, a bare moon appears in a back window. Not recognizing the perpetrator from this angle, we all head home with the idea of finding out if the offence was committed by our own progeny. I eventually learn, through the grapevine, that one particular fellow feels he has a nice "hiney" and is the culprit nine times out of ten. This relieves my mind . . . somewhat.

breeze through bare vines—
from the crowd
a stage whisper

On overhearing my son telling a group of his friends how, when the mooner was himself mooned, he thought it was the grossest thing he'd ever seen, I had high hopes maturity might prevail. But a few years later . . .

after the game
the whole pack howling
at the moon

 Gerald George

Arizona

THOUGH A VISITOR, I could see how this place would drive any sensitive person to ecological radicalism. Flagstaff sprawls right under extraordinarily beautiful, emotionally powerful mountains. So life there, if you really are alive, is engagement with them, and becomes a fight to protect what makes you want to live from the landscape's death through commercial indifference. "Nature" itself rebels.

spreading all over
the deserted parking lot
sweet smelling pine cones

A pumice mine's cancerous encroachment on a national forest preserve has in fact provoked a protest, which, shedding years of professional caution, I joined. After all, some company is gouging the mountain so that thirteen-year-old counter-fashion fashionables can dress themselves in "stone-ground" jeans! The voracious bulldozers were gouging way down in the bottom of the life-stripped canyon they are savagely widening, but we got the "media" out to see and kept the pressure on.

saving the planet
me and ten kids in a
rusty truck

Afterwards, we went to the mountains' other side to see ancient structures left by people who could build beautifully but lacked the technical sophistication to devastate the landscape: rock-mason predecessors of the Hopi.

        alone, a stone ruin
        white clouds pile
        silently

   Through the afternoon, while the bright sun gave brilliance to
the Painted Desert miles off in one direction, dark clouds accu-
mulated over the peaks above Flagstaff in the other. How the
hardscrabble prehistoric dwellers must have looked back and
forth each way, struggling to conceive a theology of adequate power
and glory, especially when the sky grew wild over the fifteen
visible, black peaks and lightning erupted.

        rumble of thunder
        quick gust of chill breeze
        a lizard skitters

   Nonetheless, we stopped at another site, and almost reached an
"overlook" before the long-building rainstorm struck. Even to me it
seemed sacrilege to unfurl an umbrella, though the wind grew fright-
eningly fierce, scaring us back down to the safety of the one build-
ing at the site's entrance.

        hiding
        in the park latrine
        rain roof-battering

   Later, the storm long gone, we found the little house, where I was
to spend the night, via dirt roads through over-grazed scrub-land
(how quickly one can learn to regret cattle!), on which, notwithstand-
ing, delightful junipers and pinyon pines survive, and astonishing
cactus clusters. Lonely, desolate—but there, such words described
attractions.

        over the dark rim
        the setting sun burns down:
        a juniper fire

        desert night sounds
        I try to hear as if
        I weren't here

 **Robert Gibson**

Moon Rise

ON A WARM SPRING EVE Echo and I were lying naked, or nearly so, on the lawn of the state capitol in Salt Lake City waiting for our bodies to return to normal. We were looking to the east and waiting for the full moon to rise over the Wasatch Mountains.

I mentioned the *moon illusion* of the moon looking very large when it just rises, but seeming to become smaller as it moves higher in the night sky. I said that I had been told that if you look at the rising moon from between your legs the illusion didn't occur, but that I had never tried it out.

As the moon just peeked above the snow capped mountains, Echo stood up and said, "I'll try it and see." She moved her feet far apart, and waited to bend down and look at the moon from between her legs.

> just stand there
> let me watch the moon rise
> between your legs

We waited in silence until the moon had passed into her body, and then, still silent, she returned to my arms.

 **Jesse Glass**

Unsen's Stone

HERE IS THE STONE he came to day after day 121 years ago.

Every day I climb the stone steps to sit here, too, on the flat table of igneous rock. Equidistant from the mountains and the sea, half way through my life.

> just born,
> my new son
> equidistant, too:

The blue mark at the base of his spine, the epicanthic folds of his eyes mark him as Japanese. Yet he has my hair and my father's hands. He was born just a few miles down the road in Ai no Machi ("Love Town") Hospital. Now he's trying out the first few days of life in this town of Chigiwa ("Thousand Thousand Stones"), built so close to a volcano that grandmother Kazuchan must dust ash off the wash before she brings it in.

Unsen practiced his art on this stone.

Day after day he came to sit here as I sit here. Day after day.

Practicing patience. Practicing patience.

Practicing patience. Practicing patience.

Day after day.

First he would find white sea sand at Chigiwa beach and bring it in a basket.

Then he would spread the sand over the flat, pitted surface of the stone, and squat above it, a summer robe pulled over his shoulders, his brown feet naked, toes splayed. With the handle of an old writing brush the boy began to practice patience as a dancer might: tracing gestures day after day in the sand. The gnats landed, sipped sweat; flies circled, landed, circled again, landed again. He hunkered down in the heat, face luminous with sweat, barely seeing anything except the vision of distant China he wished to draw on the stone. Practicing perfection as a dancer might, day after day. I feel the shadow of his effort here.

Even as I sit in the afternoon heat, the cicadas electric in the trees, my young wife lifts my son to her breast.

An old man in a boat, a mountain wrapped in clouds, a bird on a bent branch. He drew them in the sand, then as a diviner might appraise the coins, he stood, stretched his legs and back, worked the rotor cuffs in each shoulder, rolled his neck, then looked for twenty breaths at what he did. Swept it smooth again with a piece of bamboo. Practicing perfection.

> How many choices
> to get here. How
> many troubled nights
> to arrive at this spot?

All day the oppressive heat. My small boy sleeps with tiny hands in fists.

Black and gray moss and lichen-covered shatterings of rock line the hillside path. Ferns—yellow-green-shimmering, shivering, moving every way at once in concert with the wind. Jungle crows loud in the upper branches of the trees: a twig spinning as it falls.

From Unsen's stone I see the rust-colored, gull-wing-roofed Chigiwa Shrine. Inside, the ancient drum painted with red & black sun-signs, the mirror like a silver eye clouded by the coming storm.

> pruned branches
> propped on boards
> behind the shrine
>
> stone lanterns
> frame late summer light
>
> Against the sky
> electric towers
> stalk across
> the gray-green mountain tops

My wife's people have lived here for centuries. Generations are buried in green mountain shade. We clean the old stones on New Year's Day and O-Bon and burn three sticks of incense before each mossy heft of silence. Mosquitoes rise like hungry ghosts till burning *hizakaki shiba* leaves drive them away.

Behind me, where I sit, a granite column for the Nagasaki dead

> black cat steps out
> stares,
> steps back in

Z-shaped, paper lightning bolts flutter from straw ropes.

Clouds roll in from the bay. The air freshens. Jungle crows fly low, land in the bamboo grove, grunt and squeak. The straw-bearded shrine keeper in blue robe and white tabi socks is nowhere to be seen. Here he comes—startled to see me in this deserted place. Last year he arranged an "omiai" with my wife's oldest sister, but she rejected his proposal. Now the once-friendly bachelor seeks counsel from the stone lions, stares once or twice about him, and

image & poem::Elizabeth Hazen

blue autumn sky
a bee overhead
in goldenrod

the silence in
thin air...
almost home

image & poem::Kay F. Anderson

image & poem::Michael Ketchek

everything
a campfire
a can of beans

look it's clear
to Saturn

image:Zolo (John Polozzolo)
poem: Michael McClintock

pushes the massive doors shut.

typhoon
rattles, crashes,
yet one cricket sings

Grandfather Take keeps the television on the weather station.
Kazuchan brings fat apple slices on a plate, a long toothpick stuck
in each one. Maya comes, sleepy eyed, from the other room with the
new one in her arms. He grasps my finger, works his mouth in
silence, eyes barely open. Take farts with an impassive, buddha's
face; the women, intent on what they do, do not appear to notice.
Then he rises from his easy chair to make a slow inspection of every
rattling window.

After the typhoon
the drenched paper prayers
still cling to black branches

The horse, standing in the flooded rice field, unsettles his reflection
with a cough

washed black & gray & purple,
leaves scattered across Unsen's Stone,
dead evergreen needles

a powdering of lichens
the color of an aging beauty's
cheek

Kushiro Unsen (1759–Nov. 16th, 1811) learned Chinese brush
painting from Nagasaki merchants, where his father worked count-
ing bundles. Difficult man who lived with his wife at the edge of
poverty. None of his paintings sold. To forget his debts he played Go,
drank to excess, quarreled with everyone. Yet he was a true friend
to several. Buried near the Zen saint Ryokan, with whom he drank.
No children but seventy scrolls remain.

43

Two come walking on fallen leaves, throw coins. leashed dog cocks
a leg against the gray stone cistern. pull the bell rope. (scatter the
cuckoos). clap hands. pray for (no)thing, pray for (every)thing. Set-
ting sun throws long-legged shadows of man, woman, laughing dog.

> pools of rain water
> burn
> at sunset

I rise, dust off my pants. Through the ancient groves I see the lights
of Chigiwa. Above the lion roar of distant waves the sound of muffled
traffic on its way to Shimabara, or, in the opposite direction, Isahaya.
What will the future bring us? My vigil continues, even as I lie down
on the futon next to my wife and son, the sound of tree frogs almost
deafening. In dreams Unsen's stone becomes the world, master-
works of shadow glyph its surface, there a mountain, here an old man
in a boat, none will ever be erased, it seems, but abide there in most
perfect form.

> far off–a young boy's laughter

> My language the smallest
> bamboo ladle, now set
> aside, still wet

Squid boats head out on Chigiwa bay, beacons on bow and stern.

> Ghost, if you
> see Buddha,
> tell the butterfly.

notes:

Hazakaki shiba–evergreen leaves, sacred to the Japanese.
Take–pronounced as two syllables—"tock-ay".

ॐ

There

THERE IN THAT COLLAPSING SHED NEAR THE POND i waited hearing my own heart feeling the clutch of the summer heat in my throat where the dragonflies witched each freshet to its source where the worm flew on its secret thread i was alone with the light on the broken floor the mice that crept forth to leap and tumble on kangaroo legs and all the small things giving themselves to zero the sparrow with wasps tunneling her breast the moth with the beetle probing its gilled belly until it stiffened to a frost-colored stillness. in one corner a rusted clock rammed with farm grit, chicken feathers, and the plow tipped on its side like an iron shoe alive with a dance of spiders. goodbye i said goodbye the smell of moldy corn cobs—i did not know why i said goodbye. all the small things shifting in silence as the summer day darkened, the shadow on the broken floor my antipodes rushing, rushing to meet me.

> by the rain-swollen river
> young moon
> above the reeds.

45

 **gop**

The Monk's Bowl

WAT PHRASI MAHATAT, a major Buddhist temple, is located in the north of Bangkok. A working temple, it is used for everyday religious rites including weekly sabbath rites, meditation classes, and ordinations. People also come here everyday from 6 A.M. to 8 A.M, to make merit for this life and the next.

> among white buildings
> the tall, thin smokestack
> of a crematorium

The most common way to make merit is to give food to the monks. Another way is to feed the animals that live there. Supplicants also "buy" creatures to release into the pond. There used to be birds for setting free, sparrows, but I don't see any today. People often come to make merit on their birthdays and when they are having a string of bad luck and are trying to turn that around. On Sundays, they may make merit in another way.

> rising sun
> a man rubs gold leaf
> on the Buddha's arm

A policeman at the temple gate uses a whistle and hand and arm signals to direct the flow of vehicles in and out of the temple grounds.

> exhaust fumes—
> a food vendor directs
> traffic with her tray

Past the parking lot, there is a line of perhaps 10 vendors with their four-wheeled carts on the right side of the road leading to the main temple. Here the people who don't bring gifts from home can buy food. For the monks, curries, stir-fried vegetables, white rice, fruits and desserts, bottled water; bread crusts and vegetable pellets for the animals. The food is stored in clear plastic bags sealed with a rubber band. Beyond the food vendors, there are others squatting or sitting on small stools next to plastic tubs of fish, squirming eels, cockles, and turtles. Flower garlands are also on sale here, for offering to the monks. I wonder if I buy one of the pretty garlands to take home, instead of giving it to a monk, how big a sin that would be.

> lotus blossoms
> a vendor shouts,
> "Want to buy some food?"

There is a reception line waiting for the monks, small children to gray-haired adults. Three or four barefoot monks with shaven heads, wearing drab orange robes, move slowly down the line. After an offering is put into the monk's bowl, sometimes the person kneels, and the monk chants a short blessing before moving on. When the black metal bowl is nearly full, a temple boy puts the little plastic bags of food into an orange pail. When the pail is full, the boy carries it to the kitchen, while the monk continues down the line.

Hundreds of pigeons and many dogs cover a nearby grass field. A child and an old nun dressed in white and with her head shaved feed vegetable pellets to the birds. My eyes seem to fix on the one completely white pigeon in the whole flock.

> the odor—
> a man sells
> lottery tickets

This temple, like others in Thailand, doubles as a pound; people "donate" unwanted dogs. Sometimes other animals are donated, such as chickens, cows, goats and water buffalo. Deeper inside the grounds are many more mange-ridden dogs.

nose in the air—
a woman carries
her pug

Beyond the field is a pond with a strong stench. People stand on a bridge leading to an island in the middle. Children are throwing bread crusts into the water. Edging closer, I see the open mouths of big catfish as they jostle for the crusts. Pigeons line the rails. Because poor people will eat just about any bird larger than a sparrow in Thailand, I was in awe that these pigeons would let us get so close to them. A few people walk to the island to kneel and release creatures into the pond after praying. I wonder how many times some of the larger turtles have been given their "freedom" over the years.

rotting vegetation—
the neck of a beer bottle
bobs on the surface

Carolyn Hall

Protective Coloration

ON THE STREET WHERE I GO FOR TAKE-OUT BURRITOS you can also buy old Wedgewood stoves and Westinghouse fridges, new and used books, old and new clothing, low-fat lattés, and assorted recreational drugs. It's what my mother used to call a colorful neighborhood. It was there that I went to pick up the main course for a casual dinner with friends.

> underside
> of the red canvas awning
> not faded

Heading back to my car with beers, soft drinks, and burritos and chips for a party of six, browsing at sidewalk sales was clearly not on my agenda. But there, just in my path, a homeless man was emptying the contents of his grocery cart onto the pavement, hoping to sell what he could. At first glance, I thought there was nothing here to waylay me. But next thing I knew, I had set my bags on the ground and was sorting through his meager belongings. Just under a pile of wrinkled shirts, I found them—two trays of colorful butterflies pressed under glass. "How much?" I said—then paid him what he asked.

Later, after our dinner guests had gone, I inspected my purchases to see just what I had bought. They were scientific specimens illustrating the principle of mimicry. According to legends printed on the back, in each tray a butterfly distasteful or poisonous to birds was displayed beside an innocuous butterfly which looked so much like its noxious cousin that it was shunned by predators.

in the appliance store doorway
calling a Maytag box
home

Next time I went to the burrito shop, I looked for that man to ask
how he came to possess these wonderful things. There were several
men with grocery carts—but I couldn't recognize whether the man
who'd sold me the butterflies was among them.

city lights
trying to make out
the constellations

❧

A Crow Not Settled

ALMOST EVERY THURSDAY for the past four years I have driven north
across the Golden Gate Bridge to attend a writing workshop in the
quaint village of Mill Valley. A group of nine—sometimes ten—
women, we have come to know each other intimately. Deepest
secrets and family skeletons are sometimes let out of the closet in
this confidential setting. Settled into our favorite chairs, with
slatted light through venetian blinds striping our shoulders and
the notebooks in our laps, we write. We read aloud what we have
written. We give each other feedback and encouragement. Among
us there are novelists, memoirists, essayists, poets—but never, until
now, a haiku writer.

It was only ten months ago that haiku came into my life. A
friend read me Bashô's "A crow/has settled on a bare branch—/
autumn evening." I knew I was supposed to react in some intense
visceral way that I simply could not manage. My failure to appre-
ciate the poetry of the master just made me feel stupid—somehow
inadequate. When the friend offered up some haiku of his own, I

nodded my head sagely and said "Mmmm." Or perhaps "Ahhh."
The truth was, I simply didn't get it.

Then one day it dawned on me that a short poem I had written
was sort of haiku-ish. I tried it out on him.

the wind and I
pass by the tree together
blossoms in my hair

"Yeah, that's haiku," he said. And I was, inexplicably, far more
excited than I dared let on. I went home and started scribbling more
"haiku"—most of them dreadful. But my curiosity was piqued. I
made a trip to the bookstore and bought everything with "haiku" in
its title—both the old masters and contemporary poets. I sent away
for back issues of haiku journals and read them over and over. I wrote
more poems of my own. I learned the name of a local poet and
practically begged her to take me on as a pupil. She offered both
advice and friendship (for which I am so grateful). "That's it—
you've got it!" she'd sometimes say. But more often it was, "So?
Where's the haiku moment?" Back to the drawing board I'd go.
When finally I got up enough nerve to send "the wind and I" (and
several other poems) to an editor, it came back with a note saying
"Sorry." I tried again. And again.

Soon I was writing nothing *but* haiku and senryu. I was attending
haiku meetings and haiku workshops. I was writing linked verses
with local haiku poets. And every Thursday I was bringing haiku to
my writing workshop and asking my old writing pals for their feed-
back. Predictably, they said "Hmmm." And "Ahhh." And they
squirmed in their chairs not knowing what more to say. They asked
how I'd like them to respond to these little poems. And what is a
haiku anyway? And, knowing so little myself, I hardly knew what to
tell them. And I felt guilty for causing them perhaps to feel a little
stupid, a little inadequate.

Still, week after week I brought my haiku offerings to my Mill
Valley group. Over time they became less intimidated and felt more
comfortable saying "I like this because . . ." or "I don't respond to
this because . . ." But I felt like I was torturing them. One week,
during our check-in, I said, "Well, for a while I wasn't writing. But

51

now I am again." One of my pals responded gleefully, "I'm so glad you're back to writing stories!" It wasn't hard to figure out that to her (perhaps to all of them) "not writing" meant writing haiku; "writing" meant memoirs or stories or lyric poems. And I knew then that I should consider leaving this group—release them from this haiku bondage—and immerse myself fully in the haiku-writing world. But considering was as much as I was able to manage. I have, in fact, been considering this option for months now. While still in the process of considering, I have come with my Mill Valley group to a long-planned four day writing retreat. My goals: (1) to write haiku, (2) to try to write haibun (as a way to combine my prose and poetry), and (3) to finally make the big decision.

St. Dorothy's Rest is a beautiful camp nestled in the redwoods of Camp Meeker, California. Lydia House, where we are lodged, has huge, redwood-paneled rooms and arched, mullioned windows that look out over evergreen-studded hillsides on clear days, and into mist-shrouded, dripping trees when it rains. We have had both— sun and rain—and it is glorious.

Our days are structured. Awake at 7 o'clock (an hour before my usual rising) but to bed by 10 o'clock or so (three hours before my normal bedtime). Heartier souls than I are on their yoga mats by 7:30, or have finished invigorating hikes by the time I am just stumbling bleary-eyed into the shower.

> restless night
> the morning starts
> without me

At 8 o'clock we straggle to Main House for a hearty breakfast prepared by the friendly kitchen staff. By choice we begin the day in silence and maintain that silence through the morning meal.

> on the path
> the dog from
> last night's dream

> smell of burnt toast—
> in a white dish
> raspberry jam

Back at Lydia House we settle onto generously cushioned wicker furniture and continue to write our novels or our stories or our poems until the writing exercises begin. "Write down ten characters who affect your character's life. Then write a few sentences describing them and their core beliefs." These are the characters who will people our freewriting assignments for the next three days. But because I am no longer writing fiction, because I have no interest in the characters I invented (it seems so long ago), my characters are my family. And the main character is me. And with every assignment I think, Oh no, not my mother again! Not my father again! But dutifully I write without stopping, without picking my pen up from the paper for the assigned 15 or 20 minutes, and it seems like an hour, and it feels like my wrist will break and my hand will fall off. I have not written anything longer than a haiku for so long. And after each freewrite, we read to each other what we have written. And I am sort of interested in what others have written—and sort of not; surprised and delighted sometimes by what their characters are up to now—but sometimes not. And I wonder again what am I doing here.

Before I can answer my own question, it is lunch time. We don our rain gear and head down to Main House again. Along the way I stop to inspect the rain beads cradled in cobweb slings along on the fence and the moss on the trees and the tanoak leaves that cushion the path. In the rain the evenly-veined leaves look like so many fossils, or the shiny black backs of beetles. It is cold and wet and wonderful.

baked potato
warm in my hands
february rain

The afternoon (until four o'clock) is free time—a silent time to contemplate, or read, or write, or explore. I do some of each. Several of us head down the trail to investigate this site.

clay path
bootprints fill with
orange rain

53

Back at Lydia House I try to read a novel but keep putting it aside and picking up haiku anthologies instead. And next thing I know, I am putting the books down and picking up my notebook and scribbling poems about what I have just seen. And I find myself feeling a little annoyed when it is time for us to gather around the wicker coffee table for more writing assignments. We each pour ourselves a glass of water from the lopsided white porcelain pitcher with green vines crawling up its sides. We plump pillows behind our backs. We riffle through our notebooks till we find a blank page. We listen to instructions. For a moment there are puzzled, con-templative looks on faces around the room, then, finally, the furious scritching of pens.

novelist
the wicker chair groans
with the weight of her story

An hour of writing. And then dinner time at last. (How wonderful to be fed three times a day without having to give it a moment's thought!) And when the meal is over, we make our way back to Lydia House once more (this time with the aid of our feeble flash-lights). Out of our rain gear. Into our slippers. Then we gather around the enormous fireplace and read to one another—inspiring pieces by our favorite authors.

in the lodge
ten women writers—
stoking the fire

I read from Jim Kacian's *Six Directions*—both the prose and the poetry, hoping to help my friends understand what haiku is all about. Though I hear them make appreciative sounds in the backs of their throats, I stop short of using all of my allotted time, afraid to overload them with haiku and make them uncomfortable again. Instead, I take this opportunity to ask them how they feel about having to read and respond to haiku every week. When I suggest that I am thinking of leaving the group, they are kind and generous (as I knew they would be) and say that they *like* reading my poems; that they are learning along with me.

The third day is much like the second. Three more good meals. More writing assignments—with which I am becoming more and more impatient, disgruntled. The more prose I am required to write, the more I resist it, and the more I want to be left to my own devices—to observe and write my observations in three short lines. I can hardly wait to get out of doors to seek out the treasures this place holds.

writing retreat
green lichen-scribble
on the fence posts

tumbling pine cone
down the path
faster than I

On the fourth and final day, soon after breakfast we gather around the fireplace. We are each to read something we have written during the past three days—then give each other written feedback. My plan is to read my haiku. Before bedtime the night before, I collect them into one manuscript and am happy to find more than twenty. I read them aloud that last morning.

Back at home, I read the comments from my women friends, my writing pals. Again they are generous and encouraging. These are among the best you have written, they say. You are part of the group. Please stay.

Today I am leaning more toward leaving than toward staying—almost ready to follow my head rather than my heart. Or is it just the other way around? I don't know the answer to that, and therein lies the problem. When I went on this retreat, I had three goals: to write haiku, to compose haibun, and to finally make the big decision. I accomplished the first. I am working on the second. Perhaps that is all I can ask of myself right now.

between the screen
and the window
the fly

St. Dorothy's Rest, Camp Meeker, California
February 2000

Elizabeth Hazen

Here's Looking At You

MID-MARCH. TIME TO GO THROUGH LAST FALL'S POTATOES in their neat rows of bushel baskets on the cellar floor. Rub off the sprouting eyes. Save what can be saved. Most of the potatoes will be wrinkly and soft by now, especially the one-inch diameter tag-alongs we harvested for soups and stews. Those little ones have a way of escaping the earlier sortings. One escaped.

I reach the bottom of the stairs and turn back toward the grimy slit of cellar window. Spring. The sun. The . . .

Something, beginning in the darkness behind the freezer, has come out into the murk of the underground room. Thinner than a pencil, a pale self-supporting filament stands in graceful undulations fifteen feet long. Its advancing end, equipped with a bud of miniature waxy leaves, is poised five feet above the floor, angled toward the dusty window.

> March sun
> at the cellar window
> a potato's eye

image:Kuniharu Shimizu
poem:Anthony J. Pupello

Soho gallery —
in the sound-proof room
the Hokusai print

wild strawberries...
after picking them all day
i watch dreams of color

image:Keiko Higuchi
poem:Zinovy Vayman

image & poem::Jeanne Emrich

first blizzard . . .
finding the shape of me
in last year's boots

while kneeling
Brother Tim
finds an apple

image & poem::Michael Lyle

Anne M. Homan

Black and White

WHILE I WAS HIKING ALONGSIDE MORGAN TERRITORY ROAD in the Mount Diablo foothills, an odd pattern amid the gravel attracted me. The small rock I picked up felt comfortable in my hand. Egg-shaped, the smooth black matrix had four white quartz latitudinal stripes of varying widths. Through the long axis on both sides ran a rough hand-chipped groove meant for a leather thong. This charmstone at some time had dangled from the neck of a medicine man or woman. About 1500 years old, perhaps it had been handed down from wise person to wise person until the final remnants of the Volvon tribe left the Black Hills for Mission San Jose in 1806. The stone's charms could not protect the Volvons from the good intentions of Spanish friars.

empty mission yard—
a glint of frost
off unmarked graves

 **Ken Hurm**

Mother's Day

MOTHER'S DAY. IT STARTS WITH THE SOUND OF RAIN GURGLING down the water spout. I rise to close the living room windows, for the wind is picking up. But the rain is soft and gentle.

No sounds except the steady gurgle of the water spout and the ding-dinging of the wind chime. And the ticking of my clock, which will soon lull me back to sleep.

Breathtaking, the stately irises, rising majestically on tall stalks and unfolding their scented loveliness to the rain. Their many varieties are so hardy, prolific and widespread. They are indeed "poor men's orchids."

> prize iris:
> my neighbor's dog pauses
>   to scent it

 **Jim Kacian**

Grace

WHEN I WAS IN 6ᵀᴴ GRADE I won an award for an essay I wrote. The topic of the essay was "grace" as defined in the somewhat specialized Catholic sense. I used, as my point of departure, the survival of cats in Saturday morning cartoons. In these cartoons, a cat, outwitted once again by mouse or dog and suffering unimagineable catastrophe, would lie spent while we watched the ghost-images which represented its lives float up and out and away from its lifeless body—one, two, three, all the way to nine—and then at the last moment the cat, unwilling to part from this life just yet, would rouse from its torpor and reach out, barely snaring this ninth ghost by the tip of a hind paw or tail, and reel its lives, in reverse order, back into its body. No cats ever died in these cartoons. Grace, I argued, was God's method of permitting men to suffer spiritual catastrophe, and yet, by special dispensation, repent in time to salvage life from certain death. Or else God was the fisherman, willing to play out infinite line to manage us back to the net of salvation, only letting the line slip when all hope had been snuffed by death.

This was a great success. The nuns made much of me for the rest of the year, including the Mother Superior, a truly intelligent woman who knew a good fish (or cat) story when she heard one. She submitted it to a couple of Catholic literary magazines where it received a little pleasing attention and granted me a modest celebrity among priests and nuns in the diocese. It didn't have much effect on me, however—I still wanted to be a scientist.

Last week I was asked, certainly out of desperation, to babysit for a friend's five-year-old daughter overnight. She was already in bed when I arrived Friday night, so I didn't see her until Saturday morning, after I'd risen and gone downstairs. She had already made her way to the TV room, and had turned on her own cartoons. A race of creatures born of nightmare were swarming the planet, and the creatures which looked most like us were shooting them, shooting them without surcease, and yet they came without end, more and more and more until it was time for a commercial. Through it all she lay with a grip around her teddy bear, oblivious to the supercharged gunfire, fast asleep.

> station break—
> the quiet
> of her breathing

❦

Home

EVERY THANKSGIVING I HEAD NORTH to visit my mother in the town I grew up in. Like the town, she's thin and failing. This will be the last time.

> half-way home
> I miss my turn—
> the century oak now gone

Michael Ketchek

Lunar Eclipse

MY FRIEND FRANK AND I are driving through a snowstorm on the way to Bare Hill in hope of seeing the total eclipse of the moon. The radio warns us there is a travel advisory, and all unnecessary travel is discouraged. We laugh a bit foolishly at this advice coming over the airwaves.

snowstorm—
out on this eclipse night
only lunatics

Bare Hill, a place revered by the Seneca Indians, rises from the shore of Canandaigua Lake into a large broad hill that overlooks the lake and the surrounding country. The sacredness of the hill, the chance that the storm front will move through, along with more than our fair share of dumb luck are what Frank and I are counting on in our quest to see the eclipse.

driving by faith . . .
from the farmer's windblown field
blinding snow

Because of the storm we are running late and are ten minutes from Bare Hill at the time the eclipse is beginning, but it is still snowing so we don't feel as if we are missing anything. We notice that the snow is no longer falling heavily and we take this as an omen that it might clear altogether later that night and some of the eclipse will be visible to us. Suddenly Frank who is driving points at the windshield. "Look."

A glowing orb
mysterious behind clouds
missing a sliver

Both of us are stunned to see the eclipse through the now gently falling snow. After an hour and a half of tense driving we slap each other five and exult in our good fortune. A few minutes later we are driving up the side road that leads to the Bare Hill parking area, pleased that it is plowed all the way to the top, something that does not happen every winter. We jump out of the car into bitter cold. Clouds rush past, covering then uncovering, stringing whispy trails swiftly across the eclipsing moon.

the wild wind
carries our howls
to the moon

Even though it is cold (checking a wind-chill chart the next day I estimate that it felt like thirty below) we are exuberant. Frank has taken a drum from his car and is beating a primal rhythm. Wearing a parka and hiking boots I am dancing in the snow-reflected moonlight that waxes and wanes according to the wind-driven clouds.

Then it happens the last bit of silver crescent is gone and magically moments later the sky clears completely. Orion the Hunter and hundreds of other stars shine brightly in the clear winter sky. The moon glows dimly orange like a pumpkin, or rather like a lit but uncarved jack-o-lantern.

In the car there is a thermos of hot ginger tea and a bottle of scotch. We pour ourselves a cup of tea and pass the bottle back and forth several times. Then we walk a couple hundred yards to the edge of the nature preserve where a mutual friend has a tiny cabin.

the wood so cold
in the cast iron stove
before it's lit

Forty minutes later we are barely getting warm when we leave the shelter of the cabin for the blustery wildness of Bare Hill and the rebirth of the moon. That is not how we think of it as we walk out into the c9old, but it is how we will think of it in a few minutes, and any time after that. We stand in the biting wind gazing at the orange ball in the sky. The lower left edge is getting lighter. It even seems to bulge a little.

> bursting out
> of itself, a silver
> speck of moon

Frank and I are both awed by the sight. It is wondrous in an indecipherable way. All the science of converging orbits and celestial shadows is lost in the moment. There is just this outpouring of joy at the reappearance of some of the moon in its bright form.

> glowing silver
> starts to creep across
> the orange disk

It is powerfully cold and we start walking to keep warm. We finally stop when we come to a stand of pines that offers shelter from the wind. We find a spot where the pines are spaced a bit farther apart and through a gap in the branches view the moon as it slowly becomes full once more. Then we hurry back to the cabin cold, but feeling as if we have been blessed by being able to witness this extraordinary event. We feel fulfilled in ways we don't understand, nor do we try to, happy just to somehow have been part of this cosmic occasion.

> warming my feet
> by the stove, glancing
> again out the window

 **Jerry Kilbride**

Once the Traveler

> heat lightning—
> all the way into Mexico
> the mountains rise
> *Michael McClintock*

MEMORY TRIGGERED OF A DAY spent in Loredo . . . September 1955 on the way south to Mexico City . . . sweating stark naked and trying to catch the slightest breeze coming through the windows of an old colonnaded hotel at the edge of town . . . the searing sunlight in the vastness of Texas bouncing off the walls . . . the arid desert reaching the crumbling building from beyond forever . . . way beyond forever . . . and heat lightning the day after Laredo as a *Transportes del Norte* bus rumbles in dust down the traces of a concrete highway toward that old brewery of a town called Monterrey . . . then the hills . . . the cold air and green mountains of the Valley of Mexico . . . the volcanoes . . . yeah, the montage of John Steinbeck and Tennessee Williams in the good company of a haiku poet . . . wayward busses and ante-bellum flophouses and McClintock encapsulating the last chapter of Kerouac's *On the Road* . . . and , next thing you know, the old man who once was the traveler is again lifting a few brews—*el tiempo*—in one of those student hangouts on Garibaldi Square . . . Guadalajara el Noche . . . Tenampa . . . Mexico Tipico . . . *Oiga, senor, otra cerveza, por favor!*

 **Larry Kimmel**

The Latch

WITH ITS MINIATURE ROCK GARDENS, GRAPE ARBOR, AND ROSES (roses everywhere, like a child's experiment with rouge); with its neatly trimmed grass along the flagstone walks; with its birdbath (strategically placed, as was its willow tree)—the backyard had all the aura of a formal garden.

In that lawn (just large enough to frame a family portrait), hemmed in by a wire fence disguised with honeysuckle vines and marigolds, one somehow achieved a sense of privacy; even a sense of seclusion from the nearby neighbors. While outside, a narrow broken alley ran between two rows of other backyard lawns.

All this (after all these years), like the fragments of a dream at noontime. Except for the latch. Substantial as a candy stuck in the throat, the latch remains in mind, as if I'd just stepped out of that microcosmic Eden into the narrow alleyway this early morning, closing the gate behind me with a *click!*; closing the gate behind me *with all that is before time began* locked! in a single syllable, for all time.

> in a shaded spot
> the ruins
> of a sundial

Kenneth C. Leibman

Okonomiyaki

IN NARA, A SHORT WALK FROM THE KINKI RAILROAD STATION brings one
to the Seikanso Inn at the edge of Naramachi. The street goes through
a shopping arcade, where, near a huge pachinko parlor, there is
a *Makudonorado*, with its golden arches, and a katakana menu
including *Bigu Maku* and *doburuchiizubahgah*. Upon crossing a
main street, one finds oneself in Naramachi, a neighborhood of older
houses, shops, and the Seikanso, a lovely inn with its office,
breakfast room, and baths surrounding a courtyard garden on the
ground floor, and a number of *tatami/futon/*balcony rooms on the
upper level, which becomes my headquarters for three days of
exploring.

While strolling further into Naramachi, I come upon a corner
guriru with a sign in the window announcing, in katakana,
okonomiyaki. This word (literally, "well-liked grilled things") is
familiar to me from a Zen cook/baker's *Tassajara Bread Book:*
Japanese pancakes stuffed with chopped vegetables. There are four
varieties offered, of which I can decipher only one: *ebi*, which I
remember from the sushi menus at home as meaning "shrimp."

In the evening I stroll down to the corner and enter the
restaurant. There are only two people in the shop: the proprietress
and an old lady who, judging from the dead soldiers beside her on
the bar, is on her fifth bottle of beer. The proprietress seats me in front
of the grill at the end of the bar, and I say, *okonomiyaki ebi kudasai*.
She gets the ingredients out of the refrigerator, carrying out a con-
tinuous chatter directed to the old lady, which I gather consists of all
the latest dirt on the inhabitants of Naramachi, judging from the old
lady's repeated "Ohh . . . ohh . . . ohh!" In the middle of whipping
the batter, the proprietress turns to me:

"Amerika!" "Hai!"
"Seikanso!" "Hai!"
"Ohh . . . ohh!"

At last, after a period of cooking and nonstop talking, the pancake is done; it is flipped onto a plate and put in front of me. I break apart my *hashi* and dig in. The proprietress watches me.

"Good? Good?"
"*Oishii desu!*"
"Ohh . . . ohh!"

I eat my *okonomiyaki* while Motormouth-san continues to dish the dirt to the old lady, to the latter's intense and vocal satisfaction; she orders another beer. I finish the pancake and pay my bill (the proprietress maintains her rapidfire monologue while making change). As we exchange sayonaras, she extends her hand to be shaken. The old lady very carefully turns around on her barstool and shakes my hand too.

as i go out the door
another chapter begins
"Ohh . . . ohh!"

❦

The Path of Philosophy

A FEW DAYS IN THE OLD CAPITAL, KYÔTO. Today, a walk on Kyôto's Path of Philosophy, and visits to the temples at its two ends.

To the north, Ginkakuji, the Silver Pavilion. Not the breathtaking magnificence of its older relative, Kinkakuji, the Golden Pavilion. It was never coated with silver as originally planned when it was built as a shôgun's villa. But philosophically silver in relationship to the famous Golden Pavilion. Typically on a mountainside, the temple paths lead up through a carefully tended "forest," from which glimpses of the temple and the cones of its sand garden may be had.

Then to the bend in the old canal, where *tetsugaku no michi*, the Path of Philosophy, begins. Strolling down these traffic-free walks on both banks of the canal on a Saturday noontime are a goodly number of Japanese and just a few *gaijin*, enjoying the cherry blossoms at their peak.

elderly woman
sakura petals
on her blouse

Along the canal, private houses interspersed with shops and restaurants.

just think!
people actually live
on the Path of Philosophy!

I stop at the Matsuhana for lunch. Thank heaven, the less expensive restaurants use katakana rather than kanji in their menus!

omuraisu—
simple food for
the Path of Philosophy

Finally, the street veers from the canal and leads to the Eikandô. There, the Mikaeri Amida cranes his neck backward. It is said that when the priest Eikan was dancing in honor of the Amida Buddha, the statue got off its pedestal and danced along. Eikan stopped, in amazement, at which the Amida looked backward and told him to keep on dancing.

And so I keep on truckin' to the Eikandômae busstop.

image & poem::Jim Kacian

passing
the
jug

the
warmth

of
many
hands

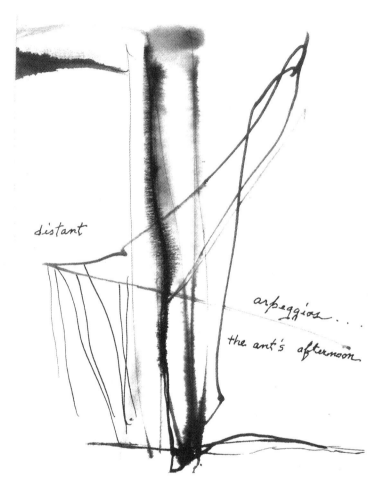

distant

arpeggios . . .

the ant's afternoon

image:Wilfred Croteau
poem:Raffael de Gruttola

even a stone frog changes shades in the rain

bent over
to its perfect reflection
autumn reed

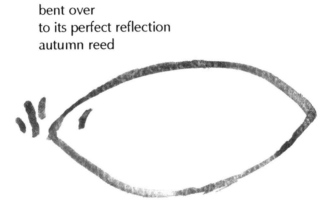

image & poem::Bruce Ross

 **Tom Lynch**

White Sands Dunes

GLITTERING IN THE WIDE TULAROSA BASIN between sheer-cliffed mountain ranges, white gypsum sand spills across the landscape. The huge dunes are spiked with yuccas. Stark light and crisp shadows define the landforms. Hill beyond hill of soft clean sand makes a perfect terrain for kids, tumbling and shrieking down the dunes. Overhead, missiles and jets from White Sands Missile Range and Holloman Air Force Base trace the blue. When kids stop laughing you can hear, sometimes, the rumble of invisible jets. On the northern horizon, the first atomic bomb was detonated. This place, a giant sandbox for my boys, makes clear the fragility of innocence.

clean dune face
I decline
to walk it

Kate MacQueen

The Catbird's Tongue

THE PATH TO THE BEACH BEGINS at the end of Macy Lane. We walk single file down a boardwalk through spartina, turning right onto a sandy path at a gap between the end of one boardwalk and the beginning of another. It is almost dawn. The air is chilly and the sky is gray with clouds from a front that passed through the day before. Fall migrants rode the front through the night and now the shrubs and grasses are alive with the twittering and jumping of hundreds of hungry birds. Everywhere we step the muted sunrise reveals the pale yellow plumage of palm warblers and common yellowthroats.

> autumn seashore
> the azure-edged brown
> of an indigo bunting

I am with people I have known less than twelve hours, and in little more than two days I will leave them behind. I am passing through with the warblers, seeking a little spiritual sustenance while avoiding entanglements. The birds have brought us together at the south end of Jekyll Island where a fall banding station has been in operation for over twenty years. Two tables with awnings are set up among the beach dunes, daypacks piled on one while the banding station crew sets up shop on the other. Volunteers fan out along wooded dune paths to open the nets, teasing fine black threads apart, shaking the nets until they are strung like spider webs twelve feet wide and nine feet high.

Warblers are caught in the nets almost as soon as they are opened. The more experienced volunteers carefully free the birds and place them in cloth bags. The novices, like me, carry the birds back to the banding table, dangling the bags from cords looped over our wrists to avoid jostling the birds against our bodies. The bags are so light they sway as though empty in the slight breeze of our walking.

> my quiet steps
> on the sandy path
> a dragonfly rattles its wings

Back at the station the crew is banding birds at a steady pace, recording weight, wing length, and the amount of fat visible under breast feathers. After their long flight most of the birds have no fat left, and they weigh less than ten grams. Their skin glows red with pulsing blood. I watch a man handle the tiny warblers with a gentleness so casual it must begin in his bones. Holding a yellowthroat warbler in his palm, he shows me how to grasp its tiny drumsticks between my fingers. For a brief moment the bird sits against the back of my hand, then flutters its wings. I let go; four tiny tail feathers remain in my hand.

He tells me not to be afraid of the bird. I remark that I'm not afraid of it, I'm afraid of hurting it. Same difference, he says.

> the dune path weaves
> from shadow to sun
> sanderlings and waves

> the feathery edge
> of windblown sand

The cold front moves on and the next day sparkles with sunlight. At the banding station I hold yellowthroats, palm warblers, and an indigo bunting. I watch as others band a rainbow of birds: magnolia, black-throated blue, parula, blackpoll, waterthrush, and cardinal. At night I dream of colorful birds that emerge from trees and rocks, sea grass and flowers. They fly away, flashing in the sunlight, filling the blue sky above the sea.

tree swallows turn
in the morning light
our white breath
    suspended

The people who were strangers become people with names and personalities. Little by little I learn some of their stories, begin to discern the fine threads weaving them together and the struggles that threaten to rend them apart. The man with the gentle hands has a laugh that ripples and lights up his face. It is sun on the water, and like a thirsty bird I can't resist splashing there. Words, too, tumble from him, tripping over all he wants to say until they pool into a place of clarity on my last night. Startled by what is reflected there, I retreat into jokes and witticisms. Only later, when I am alone, do I admit to my thirst.

turn of the tide
a gull walks the shore
with a broken wing

The next morning before leaving I learn to remove birds from the net. I free two palm warblers, small and familiar now to my hands. Then I encounter a catbird. I contemplate the oneness of fear: that of hurting, and that of being hurt. Spreading the net open I reach in to grab the drumsticks, then lift the bird toward me with one hand as I untangle the threads from its wings with the other. It snaps its beak and complains loudly, but its back and breast are warm silky velvet against the palm of my hand. I place the bird gently in a bag, to be banded and set free again.

fellow traveler
the catbird's tongue
darts quick and pointed

 **John Martone**

Bién Xú

BEFORE MARKET, SIT 30MINS BREATHING quiet til kasina comes, circles of light shrinking, one after another, like breaths, til focus stays on one, and one ring's all. then, enveloped in white, who remains? Rotating in emptiness (no one turning/turning no one) body itself a stillness in space, feelingless & w no desire to return. Heartbeat to be hear then, felt: all the hurt in every heartbeat. *Every heartbeat is a hurt.* Don't worry.

But all this comes before the fact. What follows foretold:

Had bought rambutan from market lady, not yet knowing the word or what was inside. Outside red with many spines. Back at guest house "home," one cut open, to be shocked still, stunned by fruit's translucent whiteness in its inner white shell, and white seed, white, white, white. Fruit the size of an eye. Surpassing sweetness. Sweetness surpassed.

bièn biēt (to disappear without a trace)

re
peat

the
word
to

learn
&

be
it

Brent Partridge

The Dawn Road

ALL THINGS AND OCCURRENCES HELP US to be freed from limitations—
though sometimes limitations are sweet.

I've been living in northern Japan for more than a year, teaching English in a high school and helping with translations. When summer vacation arrived, because I'm her only child and because she likes Japan, my mom came from California to travel around Japan with me. We traveled for two weeks after an initial three days in the mountain village and prefecture where I live.

We started from about the furthest point north that Basho reached on his most famous trip, about three hundred years ago. Because she'd seen a lot of Tokyo and Kyoto on previous trips, we went to places that tours don't much show Westerners.

We stopped in Tokyo for two nights so that she could meet my friend Takada-san; and so that I could chat with him about poetry. During the last four years I've helped him do translations of thousands of haiku. He found me a great job at a time when jobs were (and still are) difficult to find here in Japan.

The second afternoon in Tokyo, I navigated across the city to a big bookstore that Takada-san's son works in as one of its directors. Then, returning to our hotel—when we were just across the street from it, we both exclaimed at the beautiful sky.

> the sun disappears
> as a cloud canyon changes
> between skyscrapers

The next day we mostly spent on a fast train traveling south.

harvest will be late—
storks and egrets form a flock
and fly together

train station study—
shadows' edges are blurred
despite the sun's strength

all the green mountains
somehow pulled together
by the castle's shape
                    Himeji-jo

We stayed in Kurashiki just one afternoon and night. It's famous for pottery, but almost all the pottery was from another famous pottery town, Bizen. And from what we saw on a Sunday afternoon at the peak of tourist season, the businesses must be in trouble. Kurashiki has some great museums, though they're not large.

a hot museum—
girls plan about reflection
in a still life

the children catching
cicadas with nets, bit sad—
the carps' empathy

Again the next day we traveled a long way by train, to Matsuyama, the big city on the island of Shikoku.

island mountain
that heat-haze fades blue, orange, grey
—shaped like a wave

a southern journey—
clouds of tiger-lilies blur
close beside the train

many lotus fields
—lend their calm feeling to
everything else

mountain beyond mountain
mist beyond mist unmoved
in the sleepy heat

There's a low mountain in the middle of the city, it's tree-covered and crowned with a castle. The mountaintop was so hot that cicadas had stopped singing. On the other hand, the heat also brought out sweet fragrances in the castle; also, the castle's top floor had all its windows open and there was a strong cool breeze.

the hilltop castle
red pine, cherry fragrances—
view clear to the sea

The next day we spent shopping in Matsuyama and took in a museum with three floors full of calligraphy—that we couldn't read.

in Shiki's hometown—
I intuit his granddaughter
posing in some silk

The ferry that we took from Shikoku to Kyushu took about an hour and a half. I saw a few flying fish, thinking them to be birds at first.

in the far distance
boat on the sea in mirage
can't tell what the size

boat's moving so fast
clouds' direction uncertain
—a summer vacation

        beginning around
        Kyushu—bay after bay—
        autumn beginning

In Japan, the eighth of August is the first day of autumn.

        Miyazaki Shrine—
        protective Gods are awesome,
        chickens are happy

    We broke our journey one night in Miyazaki, a city on the east
side of Kyushu. It has a shrine that's dedicated to the first emperor
of Japan.
    The next place we headed is near the mouth of a big bay at the
southern end of Kyushu.

        happy old woman
        with a hat and a bicycle—
        road through the cornfields

        Kagoshima Bay—
        some black porpoises submerge
        near the oyster rafts

        in the humidity
        the base of the volcano
        seems all rainbowed

        every mountain
        has a top that seems swollen
        with dark greenery

Our hotel was on a mountain ridge with an excellent view.

        most amazing blues
        that I've never seen before
        —evening bay sky

the cloud-hidden moon
still has turned the bay
into a piece of sky

We stayed at the highly placed hotel near Ibusuki for two nights,
nearby there's a beautiful lake in a volcanic crater. It was the mid-
point of our journey, and it was the furthest south we went. Western-
ers were evidently a rarity. There was a lot of lightning in the storm
that night. The hotel, made of brick, may have been hit a number
of times. There was also a lot of lightning from time to time the next
day.

The nights of the tenth and eleventh of August, I viewed the full
moon alone.

the upper half of
the just risen orange moon
in a purple cloud

stripe crosses the bay
—orange reflection of moon
here it's cloud-hidden

though it's hidden here
bay's far edge moon reflection
turns into a sphere

lightning lingers on
'round beneath the mountaintop
after the moon's gone

lightning reminding—
keep going forward partly
as if standing still

before a fall storm,
currents stir darkly snaky
—huge—in the deep lake

An old legend says that if you view this lake just before a monsoon strikes, you can see a dragon. Well, I did, though not its head. It was dark and moved surprisingly quicky at the edge of where the water was of varied colors from varied currents. Also, it was very narrow bodied for all its great length—a fair portion of the lake.

> monkey's white footprints
> on a blacktop mountain road
> between the fall storms

> the moon reveals
> a nearly motionless cloud
> —freer and freer

> moon emerges from
> the head of a dragon cloud
> —next—another's jaws

We traveled northward along Kyushu's west coast to Saga the next day.

> hardhatted scarecrow
> retains more of human vibes
> —even though the birds know

> a soft slice of sun
> amid tumbled grey clouds—
> a long day's travel ends

And on to the town of Arita the next day, where we saw ceramic shops with the porcelain ware that's tradition in Kyushu. For more than twenty years, since I was in college, most of my mom's days have been centered around pottery . . .

The last leg of our journey was on the main island again. The coast of Wakayama Prefecture near the tip of the Kii Peninsula, while reminding me strongly of Northern California, is even more beautiful. The rocks that form a line out into the water at Kushimoto are the most beautiful seaside landscape that I've ever seen, or seen a picture of, anywhere in the world.

> into the bay and sun
> a line of tall narrow rocks
> —such ancient waves

In Mie Prefecture, at Kumano, are wind-eroded caves and rocks that are fairly similar to those in my favorite seaside park in California, Salt Point. The shapes of the rocks are sometimes bizarre, and have given rise to superstitions that still influence even skeptical modern people.

> in the devils' caves
> a beautiful sunny day
> not writing too much

Three days before the end of the trip, I finally arrived at the title for this journal—after having written at dawn.

> near my journey's end—
> sun has just come up over
> a very dim sea

At Ise we took a taxi to the Outer Shrine, Geiku, and then walked four miles along very hot sidewalks to the Inner Shrine. Naiku. There is a way through the forests, but it wasn't evident to us, and the guard that I asked simply showed the way along the street on the map.

> great jade stone stairways—
> Imperial Family Shrines
> hot weather smoothness

> walking between shrines—
> lily fragrance circles in
> persimmon orchard

a timeless river—
pine fragrance on bridge
to the Inner Shrine

Though the weather continued hot, we went for a hike the next day to have a good look at the amazingly complicated Ago Bay. There's a park on top of a nearby low mountain—the park's called Yamamoto Tenbo Dai. It's a place that Basho also liked.

warmth of the ocean
invisible way out there
past the mazy bay

The last train we took was to the Osaka airport—the train was purple and streamlined.
I couldn't see Mt. Fuji from the airplane, but, like everything else in Japan, the clouds were uniquely beautiful.

lovely thunderclouds
the most detailed I've ever seen
—nearly motionless

Francine Porad

PS full of energy

DEAR JIM:

I slept on the couch last night to keep my cold germs away from my husband. Woke in the night to say "dear God thank you" at least five times. This morning I heard a voice singing something like, "Isn't it grand, to stand hand-in-hand with a friend?"; opened one eye to see Miss Piggy in full wedding outfit and Kermit in tux, his green face shining, fill the screen.

". . . grand to stand hand-in-hand with a friend" reverberates for ANY poet, but it's the sentiment that gets to me. So I'd like to share some news I find delightful. (You heard all the 'bad stuff' as it happened.)

My latest blood tests, four vials worth, show vital function indicators remarkably improved. The doctor does not know why, but I DO. It's the kind thoughts and prayers of dear friends such as you.

Love and thanks,

Francine

PS full of energy

       Spring cleaning early
       books, paintings, notes
       in not-so-neat piles

image & poem::Kay F. Anderson

the bulldozer gone
        deep silence
in the field

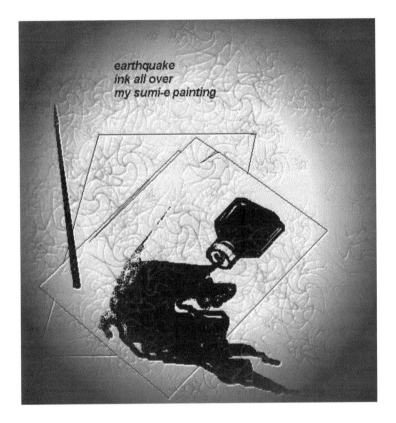

earthquake
ink all over
my sumi-e painting

image & poem::Angelee Deodhar

image:Kuniharu Shimizu
poem:Cor van den Heuvel

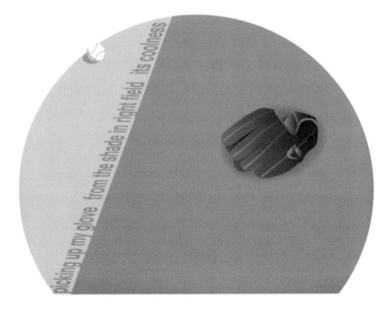

picking up my glove from the shade in right field its coolness

after the illness
sinking
into the grass

image & poem::Merrill Ann Gonzales

William M. Ramsey

Buying a Soul

"I ORDERED IT FROM A CATALOGUE," I said, opening the refrigerator. "That's hard to believe," he said eyeing it closely. "You still have that catalogue?"

"Afraid not. Don't even know if they put them out anymore." I took out the milk jug and moved over to the blender.

"How much did it cost?"

"$19.95, I think. But that was about ten years ago."

"It would cost more today," Todd said.

I cracked an egg into the blender, then dropped in a banana.

What I had read in the catalogue, which had mainly cheap novelty items like squirting lapel flowers and rubber dog poops, piqued my curiosity:

SOUL: Just in time for the Christmas season. Light up your holiday and the lives of those around you. Walk into the new year with confidence and joy. For security and confidentiality, this product will arrive in plain wrapping. This was last year's bestseller, so only a limited supply is now available.

In a while an automated voice was telling me to pound #1 for Fall Catalogue purchases, then #3 for rush order shopping, then #1 for filling the order. I distinctly remember getting disconnected. Then I did all that again.

❧

Something evidently got screwed up. First an invoice came stating that my product was on back order. Weeks passed. In December, after buying a Christmas tree, I prudently ordered a backup gift. My wife and daughter threw themselves into decorating the house the way they usually do with sprigs of spruce, red candles, and angels everywhere. They played the Christmas songs, the singing chipmunks, the singing nun, and the chanting monks. We were definitely getting ready.

    on the mantel
    crossing
    Israel

❦

Deep in the guts of February it arrived. Peering into the mailbox, I discovered a thick manila mailer. Printed on it was an informative word: MERCHANDISE.

"Ah," I exhaled in the frigid air, "finally my seeds."

I opened it and at first shake nothing dropped out but air. Then I saw it, pulled it carefully out, and stared.

❦

"Say Bill, how's about letting me photocopy that," said Todd.

"Naw Todd, I don't think it works that way." Into the blender I dumped two tablespoons of toasted wheat germ and a few drops of vanilla extract.

Whirrrrrrrrrrrrr.

❦

It has been hanging on my refrigerator door for nearly a decade, pinned now to the corkboard between a shopping list and errand list. The novelty has worn off, and I can't say I look at it much anymore.

But it's nice to have up there, along with my child's school artwork. I do notice it sometimes, like when the overhead fan is spinning and its soft, feathery edges flap like angel wings. Some days, rushing off to the supermarket and plucking the food list, I brush it with my fingertips.

My talisman, my mail-order exhalation of God.

Nonetheless I still tend toward depression, if you must know. None of that has changed—you can't greatly alter brain chemistry that is as screwed up as mine. Yet trudging out along the vacant cornfield's edge in a February dusk, in two feet of windswept snow, expecting nothing in the way of an upswing in personal happiness, sometimes I take sudden heart:

> bursting from blackness
> of ditch brambles at dusk—
> wings crossing the moon

Carolyne Rohrig

Christmas Decor

CHRISTMAS COMES TO OUR NEIGHBORHOOD on the heels of Thanksgiving. As if by pre-arranged choreography, the neighbors spill out from their closed doors to climb ladders and decorate their houses and front yards. Music blares from boomboxes, gear and paraphernalia is strewn over front lawns. Some are in shorts and T-shirts. Others are in overalls and tool belts. With a focused faces they unpack last year's decorations.

> first weekend in December—
> a climbing bougainvillea
> flashes on and off

Not to be outdone, my children take inventory of everyone's designs and get busy creating their own. They gather their friends around them and make plans for this year's masterpiece.

> up and down the driveway—
> icicle lights drip
> from the bushes

One neighbor in particular is the master of Christmas art displays. Every year we wait to see what new creation he will unveil. Soon, as if by magic, the front of his house is ablaze with flashing stars, twinkling trees and flying reindeer.

December is the month when we come home to everyone's artistry. Walking the neighborhood after dinner allows us to appreciate the designs even more so. The nights are cold, the smell of wood smoke is in the air. Occasionally a dog barks as we go by.

moonlight—
persimmons hang
from bare branches

❦

Springtime

THE FRUIT TREES ARE IN BLOOM. Bees are busy in every blossom. The garden is ablaze in soft colors of spring.

My attention is drawn to a line of bees that seem to be coming and going from the living room wall that faces the garden. Upon inspection, I discover a small hole in the wall. Bees are going in and out of it. The wall is warm to the touch and full of activity from a hive in there.

I call a beekeeper. I tell him I want him to move the hive—intact, bees and all—to a better location where they can flourish.

He inspects the wall and with regret he says he can't remove the hive without destroying a good portion of the wall. What if I leave the hive there? He says it will just get bigger and I run the risk of having a swarm of bees inside the house. The only alternative is fumigation.

He goes to his truck and returns in his beekeeper's clothes. He puts on his helmet and lowers the face shield. He positions the nozzle of the cylinder inside the hole. He sprays once, then again. The hive reacts with intensified buzzing, then it lessens until there is nothing left but silence.

tea with honey—
the bitterness
in my mouth

Emily Romano

Enlightened by Light

early dusk—
friction-sparks
of steel on stone

A TRICKLE OF WATER DARKENS the whetstone. Outside the workshop, birds are perching, burdening the trees. Calling goodbye to the sharpener of blades, I pass underneath the laden boughs. A few hesitant chirps and twitters sound overhead. Hedgerows hump the sides of the path and here, too, sparrows are sheltered. Faint rustlings can be heard as I pass. Now, as dusk deepens, a few fireflies begin their evening communications.

On the avenue ahead, streetlights attract moths, which cast eerie shadows as they flutter about. One large specimen clings to a telephone pole, flat-out as if sleeping.

Close to home, I finger the pair of scissors in my pocket, their blades now newly sharpened from the whetstone. In my musings, sparks from the whetstone and flashes from the fireflies seem to convey a sameness of mood and magic, both sharpening my awareness.

fully dark—
as I reach my door,
a light blinks on.

Bruce Ross

Life Is A Dream

I HAD BEEN IN A DISCUSSION with a friend about the vivid dream states we had as young men in the 60's and early 70's which often spilled over into our waking lives to enhance the frenetic and exciting period we lived through then, so long ago. As my friend noted, "It leaves a bit of emptiness to . . . suddenly find the mass of society practically somnambulent." My question was, Were we living an illusory reality in our dreams and in our wakings?

My wife and I had planned two days of winter hiking in the front range of the Canadian Rockies west of Calgary. We opted to climb Yamnuska ("Wall of Stone") Ridge rather than hike into Grotto Canyon first because it was more demanding and we wanted to ease up a bit for enjoying big city life that weekend. However, we both slept in the first day, even though I half woke early in the morning, only to fall back into a kind of dream state. So we decided to hike the canyon.

As we drove along the side roads of the front range we were passing through the reserve of the Stoney Indians. I sensed an immense benign presence hovering over the landscape like the smiling face of the Stoney guide Samson Beaver in the well-known 1907 photograph of him and his family.

As we hiked into the canyon I began composing a haiku on the dancing Indian paintings our guidebook described. But the author missed the impressive line of small upright figures reminiscent of the ghostlike beings painted in Utah's Horseshoe Canyon. We recognized one of the small figures as Rabbit-Man which we had seen in eastern and central Canada rock paintings. Then we moved on into the bowl of the canyon to view three iced-over waterfalls.

On the way back to Calgary it dawned on me that some ineffable something had drawn me to the canyon. I later recalled that Black

Elk's tribe acted out his dream vision in an attempt to alter their future. When we returned home I read in a book on shamanism I had purchased the night before our canyon hike that shamans claim they alter their consciousness so that they might obtain knowledge that allows them to "ameliorate the condition" of their society. I had found my answer.

> late afternoon light . . .
> shaman pictographs stand above
> the frozen creek

❦

Shad Island

I WAS KAYAKING WEST down the Mississquoi River to its mouth as it enters Lake Champlain. Situated in the mouth is Shad Island, one of the largest great blue heron breeding colonies in the Northeast. The spring river was full of muted purple lily pads, their bright yellow stems visible just below the water's surface. Then the heron began to appear, singly, standing motionless in the river shallows, as tall as the rushes they stood against, until I got too close and they slowly lifted up and flew further upriver or inland toward the trees with graceful wing beats. The intense smell of rotting fish, the unmistakable sign that the rookery was near, began. The island's dense tree growth prevented my seeing too far into the island, which was posted because of the nesting. I kayaked into Lake Champlain and across a field of lake grass in the shallows to the south and stopped in a little inviting cove to observe the heron. The huge birds were flying into the stands of high trees not far from shore and disappearing. In a moment I realized that this was the place I was looking for:

> Shad Island:
> my kayak gently rocks
> in the shallows

Carla Sari

Venice

FOR THE PAST SIX WEEKS I've been caring for my ailing mother, her home one hour by train from Venice. Before returning to Australia I must revisit the city of my youth, even if only for a day. A part of me remains anchored to the islands, to the lagoon.

The weather's changing from warm and sultry to cool and rainy. Soon it'll be too wet to make the trip. Memories flood back of my years as a student. Lectures snatched between casual jobs, dreaded exams. In the leisure hours I would search for new sights, up and down bridges, along *calli*, *campielli* that always lead one back to piazza San Marco.

I decided to stay overnight at a pensione near the station and to get up at dawn. Making my way to the Basilica, now, along damp, deserted lanes, through fish and vegetable markets. Wanting to get to the main square before the tourists come. To stop and gaze at the golden cupola, the copper horses, the statues of the two Moors striking the hours of the day.

> water splashing
> round doorways
> the changing colours

Outside the Rialto Bridge, workers take the vaporetto to the Lido island. Nothing has changed. The palaces along the Grand Canal blush at the touch of the sun.

Rough-hewn gondoliers call out as they row past, their voices gentle ripples. Locals exchange greetings and news in the most musical of Italian dialects, while the sea continues to reclaim their land. Venetian Gothic style is everywhere: in speech, architecture, glassware, embroidery, lace work.

from an open window
obliterating voices
a piano fugue

Cafes are open. The smell of espresso and freshly baked pastries is overwhelming. Must try some. The sun rises higher. Shop windows glow with myriads of reflections, shadows are sharply visible. Suddenly, Piazza San Marco. As though seeing it for the first time, I'm struck by its symmetry and luminous beauty. I slow down my pace, put the camera away. Photographs can't capture mood, the transparency of light. Some early visitors linger before the Ducal Palace whose courtyards and interiors need weeks to explore.

a swirl of pigeons
showing them
my empty hands

I reach the bank where Dalmatian merchants used to moor their ships. A large Greek steamer sailing past is a Canaletto painting. Exhausted, I find a seat, muse on mother's frailty and mine. The days when we could cover long distances are over. Ageing knees, like the foundations of this city, creak and give in. Before the tourists arrive, I savour a few moments of inner and outer stillness. On the opposite side of the canal, the tiny island of San Giorgio is emerging from a last trace of mist.

autumn breeze
a gondola rocks
in and out of silence

 **Laurie W. Stoelting**

California

IT'S LATE AFTERNOON, under fog, and a good wind. You need exercise so we agree to hike up on the mountain. At the trail head the air is almost balmy. Jackets off, we climb. 6pm, pants rolled up, I'm down to the top from a two-piece swim suit, our view, over fog, 30 miles. The August sun lingers, our shadows are long and the dry California grass golden. A little wave of pleasure. I tell you, we are lucky to be alive.

Suddenly, an aria drifts towards us from the woods. We decide to follow the sound, and come upon a small party in a deserted amphitheater. Fellini-esque. People arrive, are greeted, then pass back and forth. A woman, skimpily clad, moves among the guests. A fiddler sings and plays passionately. Someone is strumming a guitar. People eat from all-white plates. A banquet, beneath the sweep and shimmer of a hundred blue dragonflies.

> above the fog—
> nothing
> to stop me

Diane Tomczak

Best Friends

I CAN'T THINK OF MY CHILDHOOD without thinking of Bonnie. She was as much a part of my life as Sunday pot roast after church, family walks in the woods, and lazy summer afternoons listening to Tiger baseball with Grandma and Grandpa on their front porch.

Bonnie and I were best friends during the 1950s. The second oldest of nine, she practically lived at my house in the summertime and even traveled on vacations with my small family. She was the sister I never had, and I loved her white-blonde hair, her relaxed, easy manner, and her contagious giggle.

> long past bedtime
> bursts of laughter
> into our pillows

From early morning to just before dark we rode our bikes, swung on the giant strikes in the Catholic school yard until calluses formed on our hands, tightrope-walked the railroad tracks, and mixed magic potions from each other's medicine cabinets. We also loved hamming it up, frequently performing impromptu front porch plays and charging neighborhood kids a small admittance so that afterward the two of us could split a cherry Coke at Laur's Drugstore. On hot days we sought refuge in my grandmother's cool basement guest room

> playing "Go Fish"
> with French accents,
> strapless gowns slipping

and dabbing dots of *Evening in Paris* all over our necks.

The highlight of every summer, though, was when the fair came to town, filling the air with merry-go-round music, carnival barkers, and the sweet fragrance of cotton candy and caramel apples. Just about that time the local ketchup factory would begin its processing and, while we rode the Octopus or Ferris wheel, Bonnie and I would gulp down deep breaths of the wonderfully rich tomato aroma. Always before walking the three blocks home, we would pool the last of our pocket change for "just one more try" at winning a large stuffed animal by playing ring toss or choosing a lucky duck. Even once we got back to my house and changed into our pajamas, we would continue to talk and giggle far into the night, calliope music and warm candied breezes floating in through the screen window.

sunrise
carny trucks pulling out
light rain and church bells

On my dresser today, over forty years later, next to a picture of my grandmother, is a small black and white photo dated 1958 of Bonnie and me, two skinny, knobby-kneed best friends, arms around each other's shoulders. We had a similar one taken for 25¢ at Kresge's Department Store that year inside a curtained booth, on the day we had announced to the neighborhood that we were officially best friends. Rather than framing the picture, we ceremoniously buried it in a white wallet box under Mrs. Philipott's plum tree "for all time." That didn't stop us from digging it up every day for the rest of that summer just to make sure no harm had come to it overnight. I'm not sure what we had expected might happen to it, but we were relieved and delighted each time we found that our treasure was still there, its precious contents undisturbed. Though the box and picture have long since disintegrated, the image of two little girls, trying to preserve something more special than they could understand at the time, has stayed with me, clear as a calliope melody, sweet as cherry Coke, palpable as cool damp earth on a hot summer afternoon.

so many
bread crumbs
leading us home

 **Zinovy Vayman**

Haibun for John Ashbery

I TAKE A FOUR HOUR BUS from the hills of the Eastern Galilee to the capital of Israel.Thank God or G-d this time the vehicle does not take a long seashore route around Samaria but boldly runs down the Jordan Valley and ascends to Jerusalem.

> the Wailing Wall
> on the women's side of it
> more caper shrubbery

Darkness falls quickly and we find ourselves in the modern theater located in the city's best neighbor-hood.Shimon Peres, the Israeli architect of the New Middle East, former minister of many ministries and, perhaps, the next president lends his low rich voice to our event.

"What language should I speak, English or Hebrew?", he asks.

A quick Jewish mind in the audience says: "Arabic".

Mr Peres delivers a political speech advocating coexistence and cooperation. The cantorial voice reaches far and up: "A free democratic Palestinian state!"

Somebody adds: "An armed one also".

"What?", asks Mr Peres.

The next festival gathering takes place in a huge Turkish caravanserai closer to the Old City.

> Jerusalem skyline
> minarets, churches' bell towers
> no sign of the Jews

Bard College professor John Ashbery is a celebrity here. He reads his poems and they appear on the screen in English and Hebrew. I discover that he writes haiku and even haibun. To my surprise his longer poems contain haiku lines "In the flickering evening the martins grow denser" but his haiku are miniature ditties: "What is the past, what is it all for? A mental sandwich?" When the mingling starts I gather enough hutspa to talk to him. I give him some haiku books, and even suggest to write a renku together with other poets. Mr Ashbery dispassionately files my materials and is led away.

Jerusalem roof
4 AM-muezzin, 6 AM-church bells
no sound from Jews

❦

Haibun for Vadim

HOW DID I MEET HIM? I do not remember.
His wife is a red haired slip of a girl. She has a talent for landing high paying hi-tech jobs and holding them for 3 or 4 months. Vadim holds a steady job at the enterprise not far from my workplace and makes tons of money.
I invite him for strawberry picking at the nearby farm.

deep red flesh
on a whitish and thin neck—
the sweetest strawberry

Vadim talks about the major cataclysm coming really soon. I disagree with him vehemently. Finally he says, "In ten years it will be a total disaster and overwhelming misery. Everything will collapse.

109

I do not want to be alive then and you will envy me if you will be still around."

When Vadim and his wife buy a house in the most expensive town of Massachusetts, hire all kinds of tutors for their angelic small daughter, I feel less and less compelled to call them. I am beset with my own family problems. And I am pushing forward a bold new solar cell technology in spite of my boss' rejection.

One summer night we get a phone call, "Vadim hung himself." His wife repeats again and again, "In the morning he asked as usual where his rope is and I answered as usual that it is in the anteroom's corner."

Several days later I return his library book on euthanasia before its due date of July 10, 1988.

closing eyes
for a split second
eternal nothingness

image & poem::Tanya Solorzano

amidst the clear
sky, a butterfly
flares

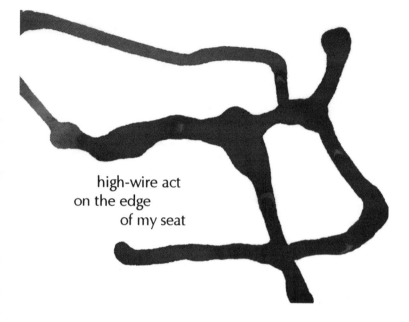

high-wire act
on the edge
of my seat

image & poem::Jim Kacian

image & poem::Jason Fech

Winter at
the summit

Spring below

Jason Fech

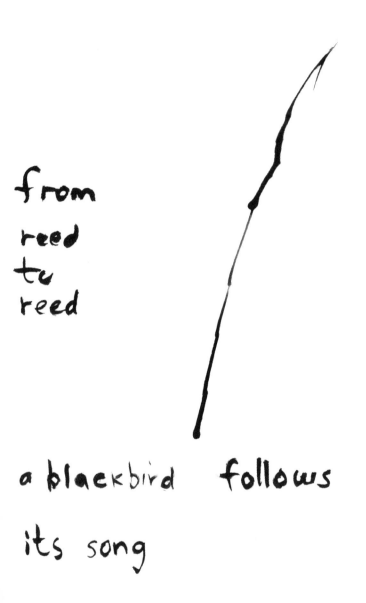

from
reed
to
reed

a blackbird   follows

its song

image:Claudia Graf
poem:Grant Savage

Linda Jeannette Ward

small time

THE SMALL SEASIDE COTTAGE WHERE I ONCE FOUND SOLITUDE and respite from the world was demolished by Hurricane Floyd. Now the neighboring cottage that once stood well back from the tideline is in danger of being taken by the next big storm. Yet I'm relieved to have this alternate retreat to turn to, and pause from unloading the car to rest on the deck awhile, remembering my first spring along this narrow strip of the Outer Banks, bordered by ocean and sound . . .

> moonpath—
> the glitter of thrashing fish
> sifted through

Washing a few dishes, I watch a small-time fishing operation from my cottage window; nets are hauled by a hand-turned crank that sits in the back of a rusty pick-up, the tide gently pulling packed sand from around its back wheels. Their catch seems slight this moonrise and later, just before bed, I check on their progress again . . .

> moonclouds—
> a man and a woman
> asleep at the wheel

As I make morning coffee I see that once again the nets have been dragged to shore . . .

rainbow of scales
through brightly colored mesh—
laundry baskets

An early walker and her dog pause to watch the baskets being loaded
onto the bed of the truck, a bountiful catch that overflows. Before
driving off, the couple canvass the beach for spilled fish, but a few
are missed . . .

over the ones that got away
her black lab
paws to the sky

Gene Williamson

Home Again

AFTER TOO MANY YEARS I AM HOME kicking sand and walking along the bay I learned to swim in, dodge nettles in, nearly drowned in when my homemade kayak capsized. Nothing much has changed except for remnant pilings where the fishing pier stood. The gulls look the same, squawk the same as the last time I tried to talk to them. The bay, which can muster the fury of an angry sea when a tropical storm blows in, is quiet. No swells, no whitecaps. Even the bell on the red buoy is silent. The sky is beginning to gray. I pick up a shell flattened and smoothed to a pale blue sheen by the surf. I like the feel and fit of it in my hand.

> the shell skims
> on the glassy bay
> ripples return

This summer's late afternoon I decide Thomas Wolfe was wrong. I sit comfortably alone at water's edge and wait for the sun to set.

Billie Wilson

Indiana Springtime

IT WAS SPRINGTIME IN INDIANA in that long ago time before television or Sputnik or even McDonald's. It was 1949 and those of us in Mrs. Remaly's third grade class did not know we were an endangered species: the world was a safe place to be with the last great war finished forever. As I think of that spring when Freddy wanted me to be his girlfriend, it's like remembering Tom Sawyer and Becky Thatcher.

> the elm trees are gone
> from the old schoolyard . . .
> our first kiss

We shared the room with second graders. There were about 30 of us in row after row of wooden desks heavily carved with ancient love stories: "MK x RJ, DW x TH, GM x SC." And, inevitably, inexplicably, "Kilroy was here."

It was springtime and all the windows were open, letting in the sounds and sweetness of the season.

> trying to study—
> from the playground
> chain on maypole clangs

> teacher at blackboard—
> from unseen spring fields
> a farmer's tractor

A serious student, eager for the teacher's praise, I was penciling cursive letters on blue-lined creamy paper. The boy behind me tapped my shoulder, handing me a folded note. He whispered, "It's from Freddy." I glanced at blushing, grinning Freddy, then looked quickly away. In my lap, I opened his note: "Dear Billie. I love you. Do you love me? Answer back. Love, Freddy." It was printed. He needed to work on cursive, too.

I wrote back a friendly reply. Every girl likes to get lovenotes. Soon, the boy behind me passed another—identical—note. I was getting nervous. What if Mrs. Remaly saw us? I didn't want to get in trouble. I wrote back, "Dear Freddy. Please don't send more notes. Love, Billie." Within minutes, another note.

This time I wrote, "Dear Freddy. If you send more notes, I'll tell the teacher." Minutes later, a tap on my shoulder. "Dear Billie. I love you. Will you kiss me at recess? Answer back. Love, Freddy." My hand went up and Mrs. Remaly came over. I told her Freddy wouldn't stop sending me notes. She took him to the cloakroom.

I figured she'd just tell him to stop. Instead, after a long time, we heard Freddy sobbing. She came out, leading him by the hand, and asked me for the notes. Then she took him to the front of the class and made him read each note aloud. He sobbed through every word and then had to stand in the cloakroom until recess. We could hear him crying the whole time. I felt awful. I had never meant for that to happen.

All these years later, I've wondered how Freddy came to terms with that event. Was he able to shrug it off or did it somehow injure him at some inner level for the rest of his life? I moved away from Indiana after high school and never saw him again. But I've never forgotten the mean-spirited results of my telling on him, just so I wouldn't get in trouble.

> this lovenote
> saying I'm *so sorry* . . .
> decades too late

 Zolo

Rant

I TURN THE KEY ON MY NEW 20 HP RIDE-ON SNOW THROWER, lower the auger and engage gears to take off in a ripping whorl of snowdust, sparkling up a 40 inch swath and tossing it in a roaring arc for yards and yards . . . clear over my car and off into the woods . . . then to proceed down my 300 foot driveway like a blizzard on wheels, chomping on a big Cohiba, wearing my crazy man hat with the earflaps flapping . . . to the ultimate chagrin of my dear snooping old neighbor, John Schmidt, who would never plow my driveway for less than $55 a pop . . .

      the first swath of snow. . .
      behind the roaring engine,
      all the sparkling whorls!

Authors' & Artists' Index